Victory over the Devil

Jack R. Taylor

An Adventure into the World of Spiritual Warfare

BROADMAN PRESS

Nashville, Tennessee

Dedication

To Those Possessed,

Oppressed,

Obsessed,

and Depressed by the Devil . . .

To Those Intimidated,

Impoverished,

and Invaded by Demons . . .

To Those Interested Enough to be Impressed with
the Need of the Victory Purchased with the
Blood of Jesus and Procured Through His Name . . .

This Volume is Prayerfully Committed.

© Copyright 1973 • Broadman Press
All rights reserved

4251-31

ISBN: 0-8054-5131-5
Library of Congress catalog card number: 72-96149
Dewey Decimal classification: 248.4
Printed in the United States of America

Foreword

The New Testament makes it clear that, as the coming of the Lord draws nigh, two trends will become increasingly evident.

On the one hand, there will be *reviving activity in the church*— "In the last days . . . God . . . will pour out [His] Spirit upon all flesh" (Acts 2:17). The "former rain" of Pentecost will be followed by the "latter rain" of final harvest. We are told that "the husbandman waiteth for the precious fruit of the earth, and hath long patience for it, until he receive the early and latter rain" (Jas. 5:7). Never has there been such widespread prayer for revival as there is at this hour, and God does not lay this kind of burden on the hearts of His people without intending to honor their fervent and frequent requests.

But alongside of this reviving activity there will be *religious apostasy in the church*—"The Spirit speaketh expressly, that in the latter times some shall depart from the faith, giving heed to seducing spirits, and doctrines of demons" (1 Tim. 4:1). While this apostasy has always characterized the false church, it has never been so intensive and extensive as in our time. Efforts are feverishly afoot to build a giant ecclesiastical organization with an emphasis on ecumenical enlistment rather than evangelical commitment. Indeed, so many within this movement deny "the Lord that bought them," and therefore set aside every major doctrine of our historic faith (2 Pet. 2:1). The subtlety and enmity of this apostasy are unbelievably powerful and corrupt. The explanation for this is so obvious. When people depart from the faith they have no alternative but to give "heed to seducing spirits, and doctrines of demons." The tragedy is, that this condition of things is happening before our very eyes without any serious awareness on the part of many leaders and members of local churches across our land. Thus occult practices as fortune telling, astrology, enchanting, witchcraft, black magic, seances, and much more, flourish on every hand.

For example, it is reported that in the United States alone there are "over 10 million bonafide witches and 40 million others who frequently join them in practicing witchcraft." The impact of this wave of interest in the occult is such that it is getting too big for the institutional church to ignore any longer. In fact, a prominent preacher has observed that "if the church continues concentrating on the world, while the world is becoming more interested in the spiritual, then others outside the church will take it over. The church is uniquely equipped," he says, "to understand and use psychic phenomena to glorify God and the spiritual realm, but if the church abdicates its responsibility, then it gives up all ability to instruct properly and to protect its people in regard to that field."

It is to this serious situation that Jack Taylor addresses himself in this book, *Victory Over the Devil*. In a masterful fashion, and yet in layman's language, he has treated his theme biblically and practically. As he has stated himself, not all will agree with everything he has written. Indeed, the author confesses that some of the information he has gathered "has not been digested into clear understanding." But the one thing he makes gloriously certain is that there is such an experience as *Victory Over the Devil*. While Satan is a decided fact, a destructive force—praise the Lord, he is a defeated foe! As John the Apostle tells us, "For this purpose the Son of God was manifested, that he might destroy the works of the devil" (1 John 3:8). In the light of this, we can submit ourselves to God, resist the devil, and see him flee (Jas. 4:7). Without this secret of victory no pastor can shepherd his flock, no missionary can seek the lost, and no Christian can truly serve the Lord.

We are indebted, therefore, to our dear friend, Jack Taylor, for this clarion call to a life of vigilance and victory. Let us pray that God will prosper the circulation of the book and bless the application of its truth.

Stephen F. Olford, D.D., Litt. D.
Minister, Calvary Baptist Church
New York City

Contents

The Devil

Men don't believe in the devil now, as their fathers used to do,
They have opened the gates of widest creeds, to let his majesty
   through,
And never a sign of his cloven hoof, or dart from his fiery bow,
Is seen in all the earth today, for the people have voted it so.

But who is mixing the deadly draught, that poisons heart and
   brain,
And loads the bier of each passing year, with ten hundred thousand slain?
Who blights the bloom of the earth today, with the fiery breath
   of hell?
If the devil isn't and never was, Won't somebody rise and tell?

Who dogs the steps of the toiling saint, digs a pit for his feet,
And sows the tares in the field of time, wherever God sows wheat?
The skeptic says that the devil's dead, and of course, what he says
   is true!
But who is doing the awful work that the devil alone can do?

If there isn't a devil, whence all the sin, and the jarring and
   hideous sounds
That are heard in senate and mart and home, to earth's remotest
   bounds?
It may be true what the scoffer says, that the devil is dead and
   gone,
But sensible folks would like to know, WHO CARRIES HIS
BUSINESS ON?

F. C. Vernon-Harcourt

Testimony

The subject of this volume was entered into not by choice but by necessity. I cannot conceive of anyone delighting to enter into the world of supernatural warfare knowing that the very study would mean to stir up the forces of the enemy. I have stated in a previous volume, *Much More,* that the reactions to the subject of spiritual warfare are varied. There are those who are not even aware of the warfare and are thus apathetic. Then there are those who are aware that there is a war on but are not certain as to their standing, either as to whose side they are on or the outcome of the battle. Then there are those, BLESS THE LORD,

> Who have *discovered* that there is a war on,
>> *decided* that they are on the Lord's side,
>> *declared* that He has won the victory, and have
>> *determined* that their walk shall be daily from
>> VICTORY TO VICTORY!

The season of several months which found me gathering materials for this writing was a season unlike any other in my life. I began to pray that God would send His angels to gather information from every source that was valid and to teach me as only the Holy Spirit could. His decisive and definite answer to this prayer has been overwhelming as it has been obvious! Almost immediately there began to be a steady stream of information, situations, revelations, and confrontations from which conclusions could be drawn. I have become aware of a growing concern across the country with the subject of the devil, demons, and the power of God over them. I have been startled with tidal wave of occultism which is sweeping across our country. The Christian who has his eyes open at all, stands in wide-eyed amazement before the invasion of a satanic revival which is touching every part of our national life. Let's face it, THE DEVIL IS WITH US! HIS DEMONS ARE LOOSE!

I would not have endeavored such a work as this under any circumstances until now. Now I do it because I must! I have not accepted any task with a greater sense of divine mission than this one, nor have I ever been as impressed with the need of Holy Spirit power. I pray that the experience of the reader will be just half as exciting as the experience of the author in preparing this volume.

You may not agree with everything in this book. Some of it is information that I have not digested into clear understanding myself. BUT, let us agree to learn together and pray for each other in the most exciting days of Christendom. The enemy would seek to *deceive, divide,* and *defeat* through distraction. But remember, HE IS A DEFEATED FOE, and he knows it, but is venemous and vengeful in his defeat, lashing out at whoever is in range. WE HAVE THE *VICTORY* BECAUSE WE HAVE THE *VICTOR*.

We have His BLOOD, the symbol of all that He has done at Calvary,

His NAME, the symbol of all that He is. Before these Weapons the devil has no defense. PRAISE THE LORD!

I have found that the devil opposes anything that is of advantage to God and disadvantage to himself. He has opposed this volume from the beginning. I am glad! That being true, it stands to reason that he will oppose and contest your reading it. Retreat not! Yours is the victory! Record your adventure and share it with me. God will make use of it later.

MARANATHA, FRIEND, HIS COMING IS NEARER THAN EVER!

JACK R. TAYLOR

Introduction

This is a volume about *victory*. It is not a work on the devil. It is not a treatise on demons. It is not a study in angelology. It is not intended to be exhaustive or scholarly or even technical but intensely practical and personal. If the reader is just informed and no more, it has been a failure. It is intended toward victory in the lives of those who read it!

Victory implies struggle, battles, and warfare. Without an enemy there is no victory. We have an enemy, and he has troops. We also have a commander and allies. The wonderful truth about this war is that the outcome has already been determined and the gift of victory is already the personal possession of *every* child of God. If you are going to fight a war, that is the kind to fight!

Because victory is our subject, there are certain areas which necessarily come under consideration. Our *enemy* is a prime consideration, but we must not become preoccupied with him. The demons must not escape our notice, but we cannot become sidetracked into total demon-consciousness. The angels have been terribly overlooked, but we must not overcompensate to the point of worshipping them. Our study must *begin* with *Jesus,* end with *Jesus,* and *be pervaded* with *Jesus.* He is the VICTOR and has vanquished the foe! The announcement has already been made and has become reality in heaven. We are set in the world to be the means by which the Holy Spirit produces in terms of reality in the earth that which is already true in heaven. There is not even room for a shadow of a doubt as to our VICTORY. IT *IS* OURS *NOW!* In that preincarnate announcement in Isaiah 61, the Messiah declared, "THE SPIRIT OF THE LORD GOD IS UPON ME; BECAUSE HE HATH ANNOINTED ME TO PREACH TIDINGS UNTO THE MEEK; HE HATH SENT ME TO BIND UP THE BROKEN HEARTED, *TO PROCLAIM LIBERTY TO THE CAPTIVES.*" He PROCLAIMS liberty because He has already PROCURED liberty!

When I was a lad, many of the sophisticated toys of today were not at my disposal. I found a favorite toy in a little piece of metal shaped in the form of a "V." It was a magnet and attracted anything that corresponded to its likeness. One day Dad assigned me the task of picking up nails and other pieces of metal which would cause punctures and flatten tires on the automobile and farm equipment. I found that when I tied a string to the magnet and dragged it through the dirt, it would pick up the nails and metal. This is a crude way of illustrating a simple spiritual tool like VICTORY.

Victory in Christ is like a magnet. It attracts its likeness. As I think back over volumes of reading, hours of interviews, hundreds of tracts, days of deliberation, occasions of counselling, mountains of magazines, and manuscripts, and letters of testimonies, I am overwhelmed. I cannot know in my own mind which information is necessary and which is superfluous or spurious. Thus, my prayer has been and is that the Spirit of God will inspire me to drag the magnet of VICTORY THROUGH JESUS across the mountain of material which faces me. It has been delightfully workable. Frustration has fled! Joy has arisen! The magnet of VICTORY has been exposed to every piece of material. That which did not respond to the magnetism was left alone. That which did respond, stands as the final result . . . the volume which faces you. "THIS IS THE VICTORY WHICH OVERCOMES THE WORLD, EVEN OUR FAITH" (1 John 5:4).

Continuing victory will involve knowing and applying the truth about our *adversary,* the devil, his *agents,* the demons, our *allies* the angels, and our *authority,* Jesus Christ, the Lord!

1. The Origin of the Devil

"There is nothing our age so needs as a reevaluation of evil. There is a need for a fresh definition of evil," said F. J. Huegel, missionary statesman now in heaven. Amen! Amen! If our view of the evils of the world today does not include a sound biblical supernaturalism, which includes a supernatural enemy, a supernatural Savior, and supernatural equipment, we will not fare well in the supernatural warfare. If our counseling with troubled souls does not include a consideration of Satan's endeavors to deceive and destroy and an application of the implications of Calvary's cross, we shall prove ourselves inept and ineffective.

It will help to know where the devil came from, who he is, where he is now, and what he is doing. It will encourage us to know for certain that his future is fixed in defeat. And yet, for the greater part we have omitted the subject of the devil from our curriculum of study. We have denied his existence in practical response to the problems in our nation, our churches, and homes. We have proposed to carry on New Testament evangelism and follow up on our converts with no thought and thus no preparation for the coming of the devil to oppose us and overthrow our works.

That we have problems which prevent the progress of the kingdom plans is without argument. A wrong diagnosis of our ill will guarantee a wrong treatment.

The devil is delighted to be denied! He doesn't want to be given credit for a job well done! He resists detection. He doesn't desire your consideration. He will seek to prevent you from reading this chapter. But remember, you cannot *defeat* an enemy as long as you *deny* him. *Face* the foe! *Find* out who he is! *Force* him to acknowledge the truth! *Fight* the fight of faith and watch him FLEE!

The Pre-Satanic State

The Bible gives us no detailed study of the genesis of Satan. The Word of God does not go into the full history of our enemy. He is not the main subject of Scripture, but God is careful to tell us enough about him to prepare us to stand on our rights against him.

Lucifer was a created being with a divine purpose. We know several things about him which may help us to know why certain things exist today as they are, and we shall observe these later. Let us look at the few Scriptures which relate to the state of the devil as an unfallen angel.

There are two Scriptures which give us some information regarding the beginning of the devil. One is in Isaiah 14, and the other is in Ezekiel 28. Isaiah is discussing an earthly king whose pride preceded his demise. He then begins a discussion of Lucifer, son of the morning, giving reasons for his fall in chapter 14. It is well to remember before we take a look at his nature before the fall, that we remember that his name, Lucifer meant "the light bearer" or "the shining one."

Because Lucifer was a created being, he was perfect as all of God's original creation was perfect. In Ezekiel we read, "Thou wast perfect in all thy ways from the day that thou wast created" (28:15). He was the epitome of perfection. There was no flaw in him.

Being perfect and without flaw he was perfect in *wisdom* and *beauty*. Listen to the statement in Ezekiel 28:12. "Thou sealest up the sum, full of wisdom, and perfect in beauty." Do you now wonder that he controls so much of the world's wisdom and beauty and makes such diabolical benefits accrue from them?

It is obvious that to Lucifer had been entrusted much responsibility in administration of the affairs of God. He had many of the hosts of heaven under his authority. He was not some inferior angel, but one of the archangels. There are differing orders of angels, and Lucifer was probably over the highest order, the cherubim. We are told in Ezekiel 28:14 "Thou art the anointed cherub that covereth."

10

This is a mysterious statement and surely deserves a brief explanation. First of all, there is the implication of complete uniqueness. He is "The anointed cherub." He is one of a kind. Second, we see that he is "ANOINTED," implying a work of Holy God. He was the object of God's admiration with a personality of winsome charm that commanded the adoration of the hosts of heaven. Thirdly, he was the cherub that "COVERETH." This would have to do with protection and defense. He was in all probability the nearest one to the throne of God. He reflected as no other created being the glory of God.

Added to this was his fantastic and almost unutterable beauty as far as color was concerned. Have you ever wondered why color was a part of creation. Wouldn't all this creation look drab in black and white? It takes color to adequately reflect the full glory of God. God is LIGHT and in Him is no darkness at all. There is no color without light. When light strikes that which is a potential color, it becomes color in reality. Ezekiel declares that "every precious stone was thy covering" (28:13). Can you imagine what Lucifer looked like as he reflected the glory of God at the throne? The stones are mentioned in that thirteenth verse:

The *sardius* is reddish-brown; the *topaz* is deep yellow; the *diamond* is clear and reflects all colors; the *beryl* is dark red; the *onyx* is multicolored; the *jasper* is blue-green; the *sapphire* is rich blue; the *emerald* is green; the *carbuncle* is blood red. Lucifer was beautifully arrayed in a rainbow of color to reflect the outshining glory of Holy God. In the midst of all this beauty he surely began to be self-deceived into believing that some of the glory was his own!

It is good to be able to play a musical instrument. How much more majestic to be one! Lucifer was not only a musician, but he was music in himself. Do you wonder that he controls so much of the music in our world today? I don't want to be over-imaginative, but I believe that he was such a musical instrument that he could break into a sound which would resemble that of a thousand perfectly coordinated orchestras. "The workmanships of thy tabrets and of thy pipes was prepared in thee in the day that thou was created" (Ezek. 28:13). This was his praise to the God of heaven.

Thus in this creature of spotless character, flawless beauty, unceasing praise, unimaginable color, and musical majesty we have Lucifer before he became Satan.

How Lucifer Became Satan

Lucifer possessed a will which in his unfallen state was in total accord with the will of God. Had his praise not been enforced by his will it would have no premium. Had he possessed no will, he could not have chosen to exert his own wishes. At this juncture we see precisely the reason for the fall of Lucifer—the will. There are five reflections of this prideful will that are given in Isaiah 14:13: "I will ascend into heaven." This was a reference to the place where only God lived. We cannot understand in our finite minds the makeup of the heaven, but we know that the Bible refers to three levels of the heavens. There is the heaven which is the air around the earth, the midheavens where Lucifer's place was, and the third heaven which is the abode of God Himself. He wanted to live where God lived.

"I will exalt my throne above the stars of God" (Isa. 14:13). Each successive "I will" becomes more serious in its reflection of pride. At first he wishes to be where God is. Now he wishes to sit on God's throne. He wants authority, but he does not desire to be under authority. Here he takes on the form which he is to retain as the "usurper," claiming a throne that is not rightfully his.

"I will sit also upon the mount of the congregation" (Isa. 14:13). Here he reflects his desire to control the whole of the created universe. His madness with power intensifies and heightens. He would occupy a position "in the sides of the north" which signifies the position of the throne-city Jerusalem as a place of absolute rule.

"I will ascend above the heights of the clouds" (Isa. 14:14). The clouds have represented in history the presence of God. His presence-sign to his children in the wilderness was a cloud by day. Now Lucifer would be exalted above the heights of the clouds. He would have greater glory than God Himself. He forgot that any outshining from him as a created being came from God, the Creator, and not himself. The glory that was shining through him was never his own, but he deceived himself into believing that it was. What a lesson for us mortals. Regardless of how bright shines the light, it is His and not ours.

"I will be like the most High" (Isa. 14:14). This is a subtle declaration. It is noble indeed to be desirous of being like God. But there was more to it than being godlike. Lucifer was a created being with a will to worship God of his own choice. He was trusted with the privilege of diffusing the glory of God into every color in the universe. Now he no longer is satisfied with being the reflection of God. He now wills to be like the Most High. He was not powerful like God and could not be. He was not omnipresent like God. He could not be like God in beginning because God had no beginning. That one manner of likeness to God which he desired was that of total independence. He desired to be responsible to no one. He did not desire to be coequal with God as this statement might be construed to mean. If he became like God as he desired, God would have to cease to be God and begin being subject to Lucifer.

Thus we see the fivefold "I WILL" that caused the beautiful angel, Lucifer to become the diabolical creature we know as Satan.

Names for the Devil

The names of the devil given in the Scriptures tell us much about his character. The reference to him as the "devil" is the Greek word *diabolos,* which means the "wicked one" or the "diabolical one." He who was the epitome of light became the epitome of darkness.

He is the "god of this world." Paul, in 1 Corinthians 4:4, says that the eyes of unbelievers have been blinded by the "god of this world." He became god of this world when the dominion that God had given to Adam was forfeited by Adam. The devil picked it up as we shall see more clearly later. Jesus recognized his power in the kingdoms of this world when the tempter showed them to him and offered them in exchange for his worship. Jesus did not argue his power to offer the kingdoms of the world, but met his temptations with Scripture.

The devil is also called "an angel of light." "For Satan himself is transformed into an angel of light" (2 Cor. 11:14). The name Lucifer referred to the "brilliant one" or the "shining one." When the devil fell, he did not lose all the qualities he possessed as unfallen Lucifer. Just how much he retained of his winsome charm, his brightness, and his ways of persuasion, we do not know. We can assume that these powers, could we realize them fully, would be awesome indeed beside our own as mere men. We can know for certain that all that he retained he is now using against God to deceive the nations and to thwart every plan God has for the good of man.

The fact that Satan is called "an angel of light" surely includes his ability to travel at amazing speeds. Before we get overly encouraged that he is not ominpresent, let us remember that if being called an angel of light has anything to do with the speed of light, he can get where he needs to be in a flash! The designation surely refers to his ability to deceive by displaying his natural beauty so as to cover over the real nature of that which he is presenting. I am sure that the devil is delighted when we learn to feature him in our minds as a creature, boiled-lobster red with long pointed face, squinted eyes, cloven hoof and pointed tail, and armed with a crude pitchfork. While we are on the guard for such a hideous monster the real devil walks in all decked out in an evening gown or knit suit with all the marks of respectability.

Let us not forget that the name Satan also tells us something about his character. The word for Satan in the Greek is *satanas,* which simply means *adversary.* A part of Lucifer's task was to guard, to protect as the anointed cherub that covereth. It stands to reason that if he knew his job of defense well, he would also know how to attack. He has best learned to do what he had learned well to defend against. His work of accusation is universal. He will accuse God to us, us to ourselves, others to us, and us to others. He accuses by inference or by insinuation. Did you notice how subtle his question to Eve was on the occasion of her sin and Adam's? "Hath God said?" was his approach (Gen. 3:1).

He is still using inference and insinuation to get his point across, and it is still working rather effectively. He has many who unknowingly are assisting him in this diabolical work. When you hear such statements as . . .

"Well she's all right, but if you knew her private life . . .

"Do you know where I saw your wife last night?"

"Well, if you ask me, I believe he's without morals . . ."

"It may appear that way to you, but I know him and . . ."

"He's a good man, but . . ."

"Well, let me tell you *confidentially* what I have heard about him."

You may be sure that whoever said them has just graduated from Satan's course in "How to Wreck Friends and Destroy People." He is named "Accuser of the Brethren" in Revelation 12:10.

The devil is the PRINCE OF THE WORLD. Jesus gives him this designation in John 16 as he described the ministry of the Holy Spirit. "He will reprove the world of judgment because the prince of this world is judged" (John 16:8, 11). This simply designates his position of legal authority from the garden of rebellion to the Golgotha victory. Jesus referred to the devil as the "prince of this world" two other times. In John 14:30 he said, "Hereafter I will not talk much with you; for the prince of this world cometh, and hath nothing in me." Earlier in John 12:31 He said, "Now is the judgment of this world; now shall the prince of this world be cast out." Jesus respected the position of the devil as a prince, but knew that He had come as God's Prince to bring to nought the power of the devil.

The devil is also referred to as "the spirit that now worketh in the children of disobedience" and the "prince of the power of the air" (Eph. 2:2). Peter says of him that he goes about "as a roaring lion seeking who he may devour" (1 Pet. 5:8). Now this is a designation of what he is doing, not what he is. Peter did not say that he was a roaring lion. JESUS IS THE LION FROM THE TRIBE OF JUDAH! The devil has to settle for impersonating a lion. Across the years he has developed a rather good "lion impersonation" act, which has the greater part of the Christian army scared out of its wits.

There are other references to the devil which would be of interest, but these will suffice to give us a healthy respect of our adversary. Knowing and respecting the ability of our opponent will greatly aid us in claiming and applying the terms of our victory over him.

The Legal Rights of Satan

Satan has some legal rights which have imposed upon them a definite time element. Those rights are exercised in two realms. He is called PRINCE OF THE POWER OF THE AIR, because of his right in the heavenly realm. He is a usurper in the realm of the heavenlies and all this by the permissive will of God. It may be difficult to understand, but it is true nevertheless, that while the devil has certain rights, God has granted to Jesus and thus to us all authority. Satan has certain rights because the authority of Christ allows them.

His designation THE PRINCE OF THIS WORLD or THE GOD OF THIS WORLD tells us that he has rights in the world as well. He gained these rights when Adam forfeited them and kept them until Jesus stripped him through His work on Calvary and through the resurrection. We will deal with this later, but one word from God's Word will suffice to describe what Jesus did to the devil through His sacrifice at Calvary. "That through death he might destroy [render powerless] him that had the power of death, that is the devil" (Heb. 2:14).

A foe needlessly feared, usually has a decisive advantage. Our foe is already defeated. He knows it. I know he knows it. He knows I know he knows it. He is a foe who has fallen, but is not finally done away with. This is all in the economy of God. THE VICTORY IS OURS, BECAUSE THE VICTOR HAS

COME. SATAN HAS BECOME THE VICTIM . . .
   THE *VICTIM* HAS BECOME THE VEHICLE . . .
      FOR THE ADVENT OF THE *VICTOR* . . .
Who should ultimately destroy the works of the devil, and cleanse
the heavens and the earth from every trace of his handiwork.
PRAISE THE LORD!

2. His Operation

An uninformed army is an army in peril. The greater part
of the army of the Lord is in peril, because of too little information regarding the engagement or the enemy. There is some suggestion in the air today that it is not good to frighten our people
with talk about the devil. The subject of demons is especially
to be avoided. This is exactly what the devil desires for us. We
will observe in this brief chapter the operation of the devil. Two
areas of consideration will occupy our attention as we assess
Satan's system, his *organization* and his *offense.*

Satan's Organization

The devil has an organization second to none. The mafia with
its intricate and efficient operation would look like a backyard
child's club in comparison to the devil's system. Paul gives us a
picture of the organization we face in Ephesians 6:12, "For we
wrestle not against flesh and blood, but against PRINCIPALITIES,
AGAINST POWERS, AGAINST THE RULERS OF THE
DARKNESS OF THIS WORLD, AGAINST SPIRITUAL
WICKEDNESS IN HIGH PLACES." This gives us a hint that
Satan is tremendously organized. Here are four main divisions of
his system. Let us look at them.

Principalities

The Greek word for here is *arche,* and can be translated either
"beginning" or "principality." We call the head of a school a

17

principal. We call the most vital fact in a case the principal fact. It seems to refer in the Scriptures to political powers in which the spirits work to influence governments, important offices, legislatures, presidents, and the like. We may be sure that wherever there is a vital area of government, the satanic forces are busy to impose their power upon those who have influence in the system. In the case of Daniel's hindered prayer in Daniel 10, the angel informed him that he was supernaturally hindered by the Prince of Persia. Some have taken this to refer to the devil himself and this is a possibility. It is more likely, however, that here we meet one of these principalities. The strength of this principality is noted by the fact that the angel had to call upon Michael to help in the struggle. Only through Michael's prevailing strength and the prayers of Daniel did the vital message get through to Daniel.

Powers

The word here is *dunamis,* the word from which we get our words "dynamic," "dynamo," and "dynamite." In this case it refers to "ones who have power or ability." Under the principalities are powers who work in conjunction with the desires of the principalities who themselves work under Satan himself. There are several references to "principalities and powers," and it is common for them to appear together. In Romans 8:38 we are informed that we cannot be separated from God's love by any one of a number of things including *principalities* and *powers.* In Ephesians 1:21 we are informed that Christ was elevated far above "all *principalities* and *powers,* mights and dominions, and every name that is named." In Ephesians 3:10 we read, "To the intent that now unto the *principalities* and *powers* in heavenly places might be made known by the church the manifold wisdom of God." In Colossians 2:10 we discover that Christ is the head of all *principality* and *power.* (That is, He is superior to them.) In Colossians 2:15 is the glad news that "Having spoiled [stripped] *principalities* and *powers* he made a show of them openly, triumphing over them in it."

18

These powers are demons under the control of Satan. We shall discuss the reality of demons later, as we are only interested here to see the expanse and efficiency of Satan's system. These powers are real, intelligent personalities in the spirit world who attack men in the areas of feelings and thoughts, as well as body. They carry out the accusative program of Satan among all peoples. They ridicule, defame, distract, divide, and depress. While Satan is not omnipresent, each power is an extension of his awful character, and these powers are in every area of the world.

Rulers of the Darkness of This World

In Ephesians 1:21 the third level of Satan's system mentioned is "might," which has behind it the implication of power as did the second designation. These are lesser spirits which operate within the context of a system of authority within Satan's organization. It is my conviction that in this area we have special sysems to initiate and propagate every conceivable false teaching. That being true, it would mean that a special spirit is behind fortunetelling, a special spirit behind witchcraft, one behind every area of superstition, false religion, and on and on *ad infinitum*. These *might* have had a field day in our nation during the past years. They are a part of a tremendous diabolical revival of the occult.

Spiritual Wickedness in High Places

Homer Duncan in his splendid little book *Satan's Strategy* states that the proper translation of this designation is "wicked spirits in heavenly places." The corresponding level in Ephesians 1 is *dominions*. The breakdown continues that we might be impressed that Satan's system is such that every responsibility in the diabolical plan to overthrow the throne of God is understood. This responsibility level extends to every city, village, and hamlet. It continues until every institution, government house, home, and person is under the jurisdiction of some evil spirit's responsibility. The elements are many times affected by the wicked spirits.

Nothing that can be imagined has been left out of Satan's plan.

A Perspective

We have before us a system so completely depraved in its nature and organized in its approach that no method is spared or procedure scrapped because of its heinous nature. No idea is too immoral, no murder too foul, no injustice so great so as to be laid aside. If our spiritual eyes were to open to the realities that are all around us in this spirit warfare, we would see millions of unclean spirits, each bent on fulfilling his obligations in the system of which he is a part.

We should not wonder, then at Paul's warning, "We wrestle not with flesh and blood." It may well have been that on that trip he mentioned in 2 Corinthians 12 that his eyes were opened to the amassed forces of evil bent on destroying the kingdom of God.

Again I must warn myself against too much imagination, but I have a deep feeling that Satan's organization includes spirits that have every area of our lives in their care. There are *mechanical* spirits especially equipped to make machinery go wrong. There are spirits in charge of various *physical* ailments, as was evidenced by Jesus in dealing with spirits that were deaf, dumb, and infirm. There are spirits that specialize in tormenting children. Others are advanced to cause nervous breakdowns, paranoia, worry, and anger. There are financial demons who possess people with a mania for money and wreck Christians in their financial matters. There are those that are trained in matters pertaining to family relationships who can ably incite jealousy, division, and deep-seated family resentments.

Satan's Offense

There is an area overlooked by many which affords a rich resource of information regarding the manner of Satan's operation. We could study the facets of Satan's work as evidenced in isolated events throughout the Bible. We shall instead look at just a few cases which give us immediate insight into the methods of Satan. This overlooked resource is the Book of Job. Pos-

20

sibly, the book of Job is the only written document of its age still in existence. It may have been the first book of the Bible ever written. We should pay close attention to these early chapters of the book, perhaps the first written words from God to man.

The Devil Accuses Job

Satan is the accuser. We see him accusing God to Eve in the garden. In Job we see Satan accusing from the start. We learn from this encounter with Satan many things that are vital to know about him. He has access to the heavenly places because we see him in Job 1:6 presenting himself before the Lord. When asked from whence he had come he replied, "From going to and fro upon the earth and from walking up and down in it" (Job 1:7). Satan, in the book of Job, has the right to come before God and even to contradict God. When God brought up the name of one of his choice people, Job, remarking that he was perfect and upright and feared God and avoided evil, Satan's accusation began. Satan implied that Job was a *saint for profit,* saying, "Do you think he serves you for nothing? Touch him and what he has and he will curse thee to thy face!" (Job 1:9, 11).

The Devil Attacks Job

First, Satan *accused!* Now, he *attacks!* He was allowed to attack the possessions of Job at God's permission, and God was the One Who brought up the name of Job in the first place. Look at what happened. The Sabeans invaded the land and killed Job's servants and stole his animals. The Chaldeans came in three groups and stole the camels and killed the servants that were keeping them. Then the crowning calamity took place when a storm came and killed every one of Job children who were eating and drinking at the oldest brother's house. The connection between the encounter of God and Satan and the threefold calamity which befell Job is too obvious to be coincidence. Thus, we see that Satan has power over nations as well as power over the elements so as to produce a storm.

Satan's attack is allowed to continue even after Job proves his godliness and consistency in the first instance of tragedy. Look at his method of operation. He intensifies his attack this time to include Job's body, and again it is only at the permission of God. He is not satisfied with just a frontal attack; he would attack from every direction. Job's wife, doubtlessly with some help from Satan, suggested, "Dost thou still retain thine integrity? Curse God and die" (Job 2:9). If only Satan could disprove the love of Job for God, he would win the argument. Job would be *disillusioned,* and God would be *discredited.* This is a prime example of Satan's strategy. You will catch him at it if you will notice:

> IF SATAN CANNOT DEFEAT YOU BY FRONTAL AT-
> TACK, HE WILL DEFEAT SOMEONE WHOSE
> DEFEAT WILL DEFEAT YOU.

In this case Job's wife broke under the strain and gave in to the devil's methods. She listened to the accusations against God until she believed them herself.

The Devil Harasses Job

Satan knows no mercy. He must discredit God at all costs. He deems his best method to get at God to be through a man God loves. He knows no bounds in his treachery. A man is down, his property taken, his children dead, and his wife turned against him and his God. But Satan will not let up. In ever so subtle a manner, he influences the friends of Job to extend the harassment in such a way that defense is almost impossible. Can a man run his friends away when they have come to comfort? Have you noticed that our friend, Satan, is not around anymore, at least in appearance and voice. The reason is obvious. He works through others.

God tolerates the "talkathon" for what must have seemed like ages to Job and then steps in and asks dozens of unanswerable questions designed to bring Job to new faith in God. God then turned the captivity of Job when he prayed for his friends. He then delivered Job and completely vindicated both Job and Himself. Satan has been doing the same thing since that time—accusing, attacking, and harassing the children of God, seeking to thwart the entire purpose of God as reflected through His people.

With a minimum of adjustments Satan has used the same approach down through the ages of history. He tried it with Jesus in the wilderness as he tempted Him when he first accused Him with the insinuation that He was not the Son of God. "If thou be the Son of God, command that these stones be made bread" (Matt. 4:3). After the answer of Jesus to the first temptation, Satan repeated the same insinuation, "If thou be the Son of God, cast thyself down." Then Satan, whose deceit knows no boundaries, quotes from the book of God. "For it is written, he shall give his angels charge concerning thee; and in their hands they shall bear thee up, lest at any time thou dash thy foot against a stone" (Matt. 4:6). The third temptation finds Satan tearing the mask off and coldly asking Jesus to bow down and worship him. Jesus refuses. Satan is defeated. Angels come and minister to Jesus.

Paul warns in 2 Corinthians 2:11, "Lest Satan should get advantage of us; for we are not ignorant of his devices." We need not be ignorant of Satan's wiles. They are recorded in the Bible for our edification. We find his tracks all over the pages of the Bible. Chafer says that he is a
DECEIVER,
    a PERVERTER,
        an IMITATOR,
           and a
           LAWLESS ONE
SUBVERSION, DIVERSION, AND PERVERSION are included in his wiles.
He
DIVIDES,
    DISTRACTS,
        DEPRESSES,
           and seeks to DESTROY.
Jesus said of him, "The thief cometh not but to steal, kill, and

destroy" (John 10:10).
He attacks
the world,
  the nation,
    the church,
      the home,
        and the individual.
Peter warns, "Be sober, be vigilant; because your adversary, the devil, as a roaring lion, walketh about seeking whom he may devour" (1 Pet. 5:8).

Dr. Donald Grey Barnhouse, in his classic book, *The Invisible War,* gives us some helpful insight on Satan's attack on man and how we may respond. The devil uses, aside from himself, the tools of the world and the flesh. These three approaches are distinctly different and must be handled in different manners. As temptation approaches through the flesh, we are enjoined to "flee youthful lusts" (2 Tim. 2:22). We are exhorted to "abstain from fleshly lusts which war against the soul" (1 Pet. 2:11). The watchword against temptations of the flesh is . . . FLIGHT!

With the approach of the world, the response must be different. As the world system would draw us into its whirlpool, infiltrate our minds with material desires, and seduce us from God, we are to counter with trust in God. "This is the victory that overcometh the world, even our FAITH" (1 John 5:4). The watchword against the world is . . . FAITH.

As the devil comes for his direct attack, the reaction is to be different still. We are urged to "fight the good fight of faith" (1 Tim. 6:12). We are advised to "stand against the wiles of the devil" (Eph. 6:11). We are told to "resist the devil and he will flee from you" (James 4:7). The watchword against temptations from the devil is . . . FIGHT.

Put these three together and you have the balanced life of Christian victory . . .
      FLIGHT,
        FAITH,
          and FIGHT!

We will speak more later regarding our overcoming.

3. His Overthrow

If the preceding pages have served to bring dread to the reader's heart because of the cunning treachery of Satan, these pages will serve to bring delight. This is a treatment of the overthrow of the enemy. Satan's overthrow cannot be spoken of as being isolated to either the past, present, or future.

It is a past accomplishment,

a present experience,

and a future consumation.

It has taken place,

is taking place,

and will take place finally.

Let us survey these three considerations.

The Past

There are two matters to be considered in examining the past in the light of Satan's overthrow. One is the fall which took place when God caused Lucifer to fall from heaven. He was in a sense overthrown because he was thrown out of the realm where he threatened to take over heaven. But he was cast from one realm to another to continue his activity. On the earth he deceived Eve and caused Adam to deliberately sin. In the act of sin, Adam forfeited the dominion which God had given him, and the devil was there to take that forfeited dominion which he was to keep until Jesus came. His overthrow was a process unfinished.

The other consideration in Satan's overthrow in the past is the *cross*. If the believer could see all that happened to Satan at Calvary, he would be moved to ceaseless praise. Charles Usher says, "There can be no permanent victory in the lives of God's children until they see and appropriate the fact that Satan was defeated at Calvary. The church of God, as a whole, will not be able to face the satanic floodtide by which it is confronted unless it learns to wield the power and victory that Calvary gives in a clear and ringing testimony to the defeat of Satan."

Let us examine what the Scripture says about what took place at the cross. In Hebrews 2:14 we read, "that through death he might destroy him who had the power of death, even the devil." I want to examine that word which is translated "destroy" with you. There are several Greek words which are translated by the English word "destroy." For instance the Greek word *apollumi* is translated destroy and means to loose off or away. We find it in more than twenty references in the New Testament. It corresponds fairly well with our word "destroy."

Another Greek word similarly translated is *diaphtheiro*. It literally means "to mar or corrupt thoroughly." It is used only in Revelation to depict complete destruction. Some other Greek words mean "to take down," "to destroy utterly," "to loose," and "to lay waste." There are others, the study of which would only serve to labor the reader.

These have been listed to impress you with the fact that the word used in Hebrews 2:14 is entirely different. It took another word to describe what happened at Calvary to the devil. The word is *katargeo,* which literally means "to make of none effect." The devil has not been destroyed in the sense of being done away with—a fact which is obvious. What has happened to him is even more thrilling than the thought of his being abolished completely from existence. In order to get the full impact of the meaning of this word, and thus the disposition of Satan, because of Calvary, we need to look briefly at some references involving the same Greek word.

Ephesians 2:15—"Having abolished [*katargeo*] in his flesh the enmity, even the commandments contained in ordinances; for to make in himself of twain one new man, so making peace."

What Jesus did to the enmity of the commandments, He did to Satan.

2 Timothy 1:10—"But is now made manifest by the ap-

pearing of our Saviour, Jesus Christ, who hath abolished [*katargeo*] death, and brought life and immortality to light through the gospel."

What Jesus did to death, He did to Satan.

Luke 13:7—"Then said he to the dresser of his vineyard, Behold, these three years I come seeking fruit on this fig tree, and find none; cut it down; why cumbereth [*katargeo*] it the ground?"

What the fig tree did to the ground, rendering it useless, Jesus did to Satan.

Romans 3:3—"For what if some did not believe? Shall their unbelief make the faith of God without effect [*katargeo*]?"

"To make of none effect" is what Jesus did to Satan!

Romans 3:31—"Do we make void [*katargeo*] the law through faith? God forbid; yea, we establish the law."

Jesus made void the work of Satan.

There are other references which use the word *katargeo* which are translated in varying terms such as "disannul," "bring to nought," and "done away with."

If this verse in Hebrews 2:14 with its multiple implications were alone it would be thrilling enough, but there are more. Let us take a fleeting look at some of these.

1 Peter 3:22—"Who is gone into heaven, and is on the right hand of God; angels and authorities and powers being made subject [*hupotasso*] to him." This word literally means "to set in array."

This is precisely what Jesus has done to Satan—put him in his place!

1 John 3:8—"For this purpose the Son of God was manifested, that he might destroy [*luo*] the works of the devil." This means to "loose, demolish, sever, or break." This is what Calvary did to Satan's works.

Then there is a blessed little verse which is freighted with a three-fold declaration of what has happened to the devil through the work of Jesus on the cross. It is Colossians 2:15! "And having spoiled principalities and powers, he made a show of

27

them openly, triumphing over them in it."

This fantastic little verse gives us much reason to praise upon closer examination for praise. *First,* we find the devil's system "spoiled" [*ekduo*], which literally means "to unclothe." The opposite of this is [*enduo,*] meaning "to clothe." Jesus "stripped," "undressed," "unclothed" the devil at Calvary. Second, he "made a show of them openly" (*deigmatizo*), which means that he was exposed as a victor displays his captives or trophies. Third, Jesus "triumphed over them [*thriambuo*] in it." This is the same word used in 2 Corinthians 2:14, "Now thanks be to God which always causeth us to triumph [*thriambuo*] in Christ." Examine the verse again at a glance. Satan has been . . .

STRIPPED,

MADE A SHOW OF OPENLY,

and TRIUMPHED OVER!

We have seen what happened to Satan at Calvary. Let us look briefly in contrast at what happened to us there. Conybeare translates Colossians 1:13 thusly, "HE HATH DELIVERED US FROM THE DOMINION OF DARKNESS AND TRANSPLANTED US INTO THE KINGDOM OF HIS BELOVED SON." Thus, we have been rescued from the devil's hand and *removed* from the devil's power. We have been delivered from a dual bondage . . . sin's slavery and Satan's authority.

When Jesus came to the earth, he was in Satan's territory. He had *come* to *overcome* Satan on his own grounds. That has been done! While we live in the middle of this world system, we have authority over it. We not only have been released on the negative side, but we have been translated on the positive side to a new kingdom, the kingdom of Christ. We are citizens of a KINGDOM within a kingdom which is greater than that kingdom.

Every credential of authority which Satan possessed was stripped from him by the Son of God. When Jesus went into the Holy of Holies not made with hands and poured his blood out before the presence of the Father, the Supreme Court of the Universe acknowledged the sacrifice and proclaimed the debt paid. Furthermore that Supreme Court validated the LEGAL

DEFEAT OF SATAN! He has no more right to rule because he possesses no authority to do so. Our Savior, the Lord Jesus Christ has it all! (Matt. 28:18).

The Present

The overthrow of Satan is *present* in its implication, because of the permanency of his past defeat. His defeat did not remove him from the picture. He is still very much with us. His past *defeat* assures Christ's present *domination* of him. He is both a *defeated* foe and a *dominated* foe. He is *vanquished* but not *vanished, present* but not *prevailing, active* but not *able* to overcome.

Which would you rather have, a foe that had been defeated and destroyed or a foe that had been defeated and made subject to you? The answer is obvious! In the latter case, we are doubly advantaged, having a defeated foe as our servant with all his abilities at our disposal. This is exactly the case with Satan. He is subject to Jesus and thus subject to us. Whatever he does, regardless of its original intention, will work good in the life of the obedient child of God.

Satan is being overthrown in the battlefields of this world where believers have learned the truth about their enemy being a defeated foe.

The Future

The future overthrow of Satan will find a total consumation of victory over him. This final consumation will come in three stages. First, the devil and his angels will be barred from any further access to heaven. In Revelation 12:7-9 we find, "And there was war in heaven; Michael and his angels fought against the dragon; and the dragon fought and his angels, and prevailed not; neither was their place found anymore in heaven. And the great dragon was cast out; that old serpent, called the Devil and Satan, which deceiveth the whole world; he was cast out into the earth, and his angels were cast out with him." This is the first of a series of three great, critical clashes between the forces of Satan and the Lord.

Second, a great angel will bind Satan in chains and cast him into the bottomless pit. "And I saw an angel come down from heaven, having a key to the bottomless pit, and a great chain in his hand. And he laid hold on the dragon, that old serpant, which is the Devil, and Satan, and bound him for a thousand years. And cast him into the bottomless pit, and shut him up, and set a seal on him, that he should deceive the nations no more, till the thousand years should be fulfilled; and after that he must be loosed a little season" (Rev. 20:1-3). What a progressive humiliation the devil will be subjected to in the final consumation of his defeat!

Thirdly, and finally, after the thousand years are up, Satan will be loosed from the pit for a season only to face the hosts of the Lord in the Battle of Armageddon and total defeat. He then with all his own will be cast into the lake of fire and brimstone and tormented day and night for ever and ever (Rev. 20:10).

Satan knows of his defeat, past, present, and future and trembles before what he believes. He cannot deny, but he can bitterly oppose, contest, argue, and struggle only to be overcome. Praise the Lord!

4. Our Overcoming

Because the Savior has overcome the devil, we have overcome the devil. His overcoming becomes our overcoming. As he substituted for us in death, now he substitutes for us in life. Just as we accepted his death for our *wickedness,* we now accept his life for our *weakness*.

All that we have studied in the previous chapters regarding the victory of Jesus over Satan becomes real when applied in daily warfare. God has allowed us to face a real enemy so that we might be "more than conquerors." We can overcome because the devil has been overcome. We have the victory because the Victor has won it and has given us both the victory and himself, the Victor.

As we discuss the joyous privilege of entering into the already-won victory of Calvary, let us not forget that this is but one of the side benefits of the greatest reasons for rejoicing, that our names are written in heaven. Do you remember when the disciples had their first taste of victory over the demons? They came back with rejoicing, saying, "Lord, even the devils [demons] are subject to us through thy name." Jesus then replied, "I beheld Satan as lightning fall from heaven. Behold, I give unto you power to tread on serpents and scorpions, and over all the power of the enemy; and nothing shall by any means hurt you. Notwithstanding in this rejoice not, that the spirits are subject to you; but rather REJOICE, BECAUSE YOUR NAMES ARE WRITTEN IN HEAVEN" (Luke 10:17-19).

We shall observe four facets of our overcoming: *Establishing* a good defense, *enforcing* Calvary's victory, *exerting* our authority and *entering* into future victory NOW.

Establishing a Good Defense

"Neither give place to the devil!" (Eph. 4:27), is Paul's summary advice regarding our relationship. "Fill up and crowd out. Leave no room for the devil. Have no time and no place for him. Vacant places invite him. The devil loves a vacuum. A very busy person himself, he does his biggest business with those who have no business. Keep him out by prepossession. Keep him out, nose, head, and all. Give him an inch and he will take a mile" (E. M. Bounds, *Satan, His Personality, Power, and Overthrow*).

The best start on a good offense is a good defense. Paul's warning was occasioned by a discussion of anger in the Christian's life. We cannot engage in anything that would give the devil breathing space. There are three important factors to a good defense in the warfare in the spirit realm. The first of these is *giving no room to the enemy.*

The second factor is *being sober and watchful.* Peter issues a

31

severe warning, "Be sober, be vigilant [wakeful or watchful]; because your adversary, the devil, as a roaring lion, walketh about, seeking whom he may devour" (1 Pet. 5:8). We are to remain on constant watch. We cannot be too careful. This verse should read, "Be continuously always sober and vigilant." These two words that appear in English as "sober" and "vigilant" are not as close as they appear to be. They contain directions in two vital areas of our lives.

The first "be sober," has to do with moral character. We are to be serious in character, free from greed and quick passions. This sobriety must have no weak places where the devil could walk in. He is stalking his prey like a lion. If there is a weak place in the character, he will eventually find it. Nothing will cause weakness to surface like a confrontation with the devil. A man with a quick temper is a ready target for the devil. He may be moral and honest, but the devil will surely defeat him in the temper area. There can be no area unguarded in facing the foe.

Then there is the call to be vigilant. This involves an extension of a serious character into a serious curriculum of careful living. We are to have our eyes open all about. We are to be cautious, attentive, and wakeful.

The third factor in a good spiritual defense is *resisting the devil*. Both James and Peter agree that this is the way that the devil must be handled. We are not encouraged to flee the devil, but to resist him. "Whom resist steadfast in the faith" (1 Pet. 5:9). This is to be a continuing resistance girded by a stability of total yieldedness to Christ. That is faith! James promises, "Resist the devil and he will flee from you" (James 4:7). The same word in the Greek [*anathistemi*] is used in both passages, which means "to set over against." It has the implication of refusing to tolerate the devil at all, making no concession, meeting the devil only to fight him, talking to him only to resist him. We have no time to argue or palaver with the enemy. He would engage us in compromising discussion or meditation, but this leads only to defeat.

32

Charles Usher, in *Satan a Defeated Foe*, says, "At the cross Jesus destroyed all Satan's legal rights over man and over this earth. But the battle began before Calvary. In the wilderness the conflict commenced in earnest, and Christ conquered on two points. He refused to yield any obedience to Satan's commands . . . this Adam failed to do . . . and He refused to act apart from God His Father. 'I came not to mine own will.' This oneness with His Father's will was maintained, and hence he conquered." Just as Jesus conquered through obedience to Calvary, so must we conquer on the same basis.

There is a real sense in which Calvary is eternal. It always has been and always will be. It is a principle set in motion long before the historical Calvary. It is the principle of life out of death, of life through death. Abraham won the victory through the principle of Calvary—death to self and life to God. This was true of John the Baptist as well. His life was short but entirely successful because as he decreased Christ increased. His life shone like a meteor long enough to turn the lights on the Son of God and then burned out.

The principle of Calvary applied to our lives will aid in enforcing its victory over the enemy. This is in reality the first step. Jesus has called us to deny ourselves, TAKE UP THE CROSS, DAILY and follow him (Luke 9:23). This simply means to choose against the self life and take death as a fact—death to wealth, plans, ideas, family, health, and every other thing. If you are not overcoming in a certain area it may be that you have not applied the cross principle to that area. Give your family to God, yield your finances to him, take back all wrong attitudes toward money, refuse all offers of the world, and determine only to be His.

Enforce Calvary's victory in the church. This is His blood-bought bride. She will be His without spot or wrinkle. We must stand against the trends which are inspired in hell to cripple and weaken the church in its decisive ministry to our world. Enforce

Calvary's victory in the home. Stand against relaxed discipline, material priorities, and loose moral codes. Enforce Calvary's victory in the individual life. The only person who cannot be bought out is the one who is already sold out. Listen to Paul as he gives the market report of a sold-out life. "But God forbid that I glory save in the cross of our Lord Jesus Christ, by whom the world is crucified unto me and I unto the world. From henceforth let no man trouble me; for I bear in my body the marks of the Lord Jesus" (1 Thess. 5:17). These were the marks of death—the marks of a sold-out servant.

Enforce Calvary's victory in the life of the nation. Jesus conquered the devil at the cross; thus the devil is not the rightful owner of this world. Yet he is acting very much like he is. We have authority to contest the hold the devil has on our world and remove him from the strongholds.

We are not battling communism, intellectualism, pornography, violence, and anarchy. These are but areas over which Satan has assigned his evil spirits to torment our world. We must stand against them in Calvary's victory. The church advancing under the victory of the cross will ever hinder Satan's activities as long as the church is in the earth.

Exerting Our Authority

I have dealt with the authority of the believer in the volume *Much More*. I will not repeat that study here. It is this area that we need to live as we establish and exert Calvary victory. One verse will suffice here, Luke 4:18, "The Spirit of the Lord is upon me, because he hath anointed me to preach the gospel to the poor; he hath sent me to heal the broken hearted, to preach deliverance to the captives, and recovering sight to the blind, to set at liberty them that are bruised." Swiftly let us look at the *demand* for that authority, the *delegation* of that authority, the *dynamics* of the authoriy, and the *domain* of that authority.

The *demand* for authority is to be found in the condition of the world. In this verse is simply a list of conditions imposed by the god of this world. Folks are poor because they have been

34

robbed by him who came to steal, that is the devil. They are *broke, broken-hearted, bound, blind,* and *bruised* because of the work of the devil. We do not fight against flesh and blood, therefore *welfare* is not *warfare.* It will demand spiritual authority to call the devil to attention.

The *delegation* of authority comes from the "uponness" of the Spirit. "The Spirit of the Lord is upon me, because he has anointed me." We need no more credential than this to face the foe!

The *dynamics* of that authority reflect themselves in preaching,

   encouraging the brokenhearted,

      proclaiming deliverance,

recovering sight,

   and liberating from circumstances.

The *domain* of that authority covers all areas of need and everybody in need. A careful study of these designations will reveal that no one is left out.

It includes the poor,

   the brokenhearted,

the oppressed captives,

   the blind,

     and the circumstantially bruised.

Poverty, disappointment, despair, blindness, and bruisedness are but strongholds built by Satan to incarcerate the millions in this world. We can exert our authority and let the oppressed go free! Praise the Lord!

Entering into Future Victory Now

We have been informed that the ultimate tools in the final overthrow in which the devil and his angels are removed from heaven are "the blood of the Lamb, the word of their testimony, and the fact that they loved not their lives unto the death" (Rev. 12:11). Allow me to assume that the name of Jesus is an indispensable tool in this battle and adding these three discuss them as the means of having "then" victory "now"!

The Name

Jesus gives us legal right to use His name.

John 14:13—"And whatsoever ye shall ask in my name, that will I do that the Father may be glorified in the Son."

John 16:24—"Hitherto, ye have asked nothing in my name; Ask and receive that your joy may be full."

What does it mean to use His name? The Amplified New Testament gives us a hint. It has in parentheses "presenting all that He is." Do you see the implications of that? Look at the following examples:

"Father, I ask this prayer PRESENTING ALL THAT JESUS IS."

"Satan, I take my stand against you PRESENTING ALL THAT JESUS IS."

"Demons, I dismiss you PRESENTING ALL THAT JESUS IS."

"I claim healing for my body PRESENTING ALL THAT JESUS IS."

"I confess this sin and claim forgiveness PRESENTING ALL THAT JESUS IS."

It means that we are acting in Christ's stead with full right to do so. Kenyon says, "When we pray in Jesus' name, we are taking the place of the absent Christ; we are using His name, using His authority to carry out His will on earth." The use of the name of Jesus takes the victory past and victory future and pulls them into VICTORY NOW! The name of Jesus presents all that Jesus *IS*.

The Blood

The blood of Jesus presents all that Jesus *did*. It is a symbol of the love of God which fashioned Calvary. It is a symbol of the finished work which finished the devil. It is a symbol of the life of Jesus. Life is in the blood. He poured out His life that we might have life. It is a symbol of cleansing. "The blood of Jesus Christ, his Son, cleanseth us from all sin" (1 John 1:7). The destroyer angel in Egypt could not get by the blood into a house thus covered. Satan cannot break through the barrier of the blood because behind the blood is the life and power of Christ Himself.

To be under the blood is to be included under Calvary's victory. That victory is final. Mention of the blood updates the victory ancient won on Calvary. The blood reminds the devil of the greatest mistake he ever made, the perpetration of Calvary from the human side. He did it not knowing that he was cooperating with God's eternal plan. As long as the blood of Christ is between us and Satan, he cannot touch us.

It is by the blood that we have been bought.

It is by the blood that we stand protected.

It is by the blood that we have access into the Holy of Holies.

It is by the blood that we are continually cleansed.

If by the *blood of the Lamb* that *ultimate* victory is to be won, then it is logical to assume that *immediate* victory can be unceasingly obtained in the same manner.

The Word of Testimony

"They overcame him by the word of their testimony" is a simple reference to our twofold resource in the *written* testimony, the Word of God, the Bible, and the *experienced* testimony supported by the Word. As we give witness, the devil is defeated. A witness is one who gives helpful evidence. In this case he is one who extend the written Word of God to a demonstration in human flesh. We are to witness the truth! We are to tell our testimony based on the truths in the Word of God.

We are to witness to the devil, to the Lord, to the lost, to each other, and to ourselves. If we let up on our testimony for a moment, the devil will begin giving his false testimony. The next thing you know we will be listening to him and repeating what he is telling you. The only alternative to that is to be preoccupied with the testimony that is ours undergirded by the Word of God.

Here is one of the greatest weapons against the devil. Here is in an indication of an abandoned life. Most of our worries stem from the fact that we love our lives. Most of our resentments arise from the same direction. Our fears are born in the same nursery. If we love our lives, we will fear death and that fear will be used by the devil to intimidate us.

In the face of death they were not moved by a fear of death. How are you going to threaten a man who is not afraid of that with which you are threatening him? The answer is . . . you cannot! Man has been in bondage to the fear of death (Heb. 2: 15). There is no need to fear it now. Its stinger is removed. Its victory is gone! How can we get over the fear of death? The best way to answer that is to find out how Paul got over it. Look at some key statements that Paul made with regard to death.

> 2 Corinthians 1:9—"But we had the sentence of death in ourselves, that we should not trust in ourselves, but in God which raiseth the dead."

Paul had set his face on an unchanging course. Death did not bother him because he had already taken death to himself when he had decided to follow Christ. Those committed to Christ are committed to the cross and thus "have the sentence of death to themselves."

> 2 Corinthians 4:10—"Always bearing about in the body the dying of the Lord Jesus, that the life also of Jesus might be made manifest in our mortal flesh."

It is only as Paul lined himself up with the death of Jesus and reckoned himself dead that the life of Christ was fully manifest. When this was done in Paul, he feared physical death none at all. As we declare the same thing, "reckoning ourselves dead indeed unto sin, but alive unto God through Jesus Christ" (Rom. 6:11), we shall find physical death no threat at all. How can you effectively kill a dead man? Take this weapon of the fear of death out of the hand of the devil and he is greatly handicapped.

"Overcome by the fearlessness of overcomers . . ." That is the story of the devil. I challenge you to "love not your life even in the threat of death" and thus gain a decisive victory over Satan, NOW!

Believer, let me suggest in conclusion that you try your weapons. Come against the enemy with the name of Jesus, His blood, your testimony, and an abandoned life. You will discover the victory delivered by these to be sweet and constant. Blessed is he that overcomes!

5. The Reality of Demons

As already stated, a study of the devil will reveal that he is head of a system involving millions of spirit beings with varying levels of power, responsibility, and influence. I must take a moment to share with you my testimony of how I began the study which led to the writing of this volume.

A Testimony

A few years ago the Holy Spirit began to move in mighty fashion in the church where I am pastor. In the wake of that moving were some of the most unusual problems which did not seem to be explainable in terms of mere humanity. I had done some study in the area of the devil and had been practicing resistance as the Bible commanded for some time. The book *Dealing with the Devil* by C. S. Lovett had fallen into my hands and I had given it a casual going over, but had not fully digested its contents.

Some of the happenings caused me to remember some of the suggestions that Mr. Lovett made in his very practical volume. It was not long before a couple came to me and asked permission to lead a study group on Sunday evenings using the book by Lovett as a text for the study. I gave my permission and the next thing I heard was that they were experiencing a strange and new kind of oppression. The husband, a fine deacon in our church, backed off and postponed the plans for teaching the book as he had intended.

The wife came to me in such distress that I became alarmed. She was (and still is) one of the finest Christians in our church, very stable emotionally. She began to pour out her heart as she described what she was going through. She knew that their intentions to teach the book were connected with this oppression. This was the witness of my heart as well. I came against the devil as best I knew, and she experienced a freedom that was satisfying.

This was all frighteningly new to me. I have always been cautious of this particular area of study and practice. (Sometimes downright suspicious!) Not long before that I would have rated someone who talked about demons (much less someone who claimed to talk to them) on the same level as the fellow who thought he was a poached egg or Napoleon Bonaparte.

Well, I could not get this off my mind. There must have been good reason for the devil to have so vigorously contested the teaching of a book about himself. I was led of the Lord to begin to teach the book myself. The results were instantaneous and delightful. The devil threw fit after fit. The folks involved in the study gave testimony after testimony of Satan attacks which they had not at all experienced in the past. To their delight they found that the principles in the book of resistance in Jesus' name really worked. After the studying through the book once, we repeated the same process with continued delightful results.

I was delighted to find that Mr. Lovett made the suggestion that we leave demons alone for the time being. That was exactly what I intended to do for good. But, I found that this was impossible. I asked the Lord to begin to teach me. There were times when I wished, in a manner, that I had not prayed that prayer! God began to expose me to books, people, and experiences which almost literally blew my mind. I would receive some revelation that simply countered all that my culture and system had taught and lived in relative shock for a period of time. WHERE HAD THE DEMONS BEEN? Perhaps a better question was, "WHERE HAD I BEEN?" I found out later on that the demons had been around all the time!

This chapter could not have been written two years ago. It was not necessarily that I did not believe the things that I am writing down. I simply had given them very little consideration. Needless to say, we were led by the Lord into a study of the whole spectrum of spirit warfare. We know that there are pitfalls in such a study, not the least of which is becoming so obsessed with the warfare to the neglect of the Lord Jesus Himself. We also know that there is a necessity of knowing something of the devil and his demons if we are going to live triumphantly in the midst of the warfare.

Up until this chapter we have had a fairly traditional approach. This is where the much-traveled road of tradition narrows down to the narrow lanes of little-traveled biblical truth. We certainly do not lack for maps on this journey, but we cannot expect to find any superhighways out here.

There is much in the Bible about our subject and even much in ancient literature, with a sudden revival of writing on it in our generation. But, even now, when one begins to discuss it as a reality in the midst of our intellectual and religious sophistication, he will find himself carrying on a private conversation with himself. It's worst than bad breath!

It will not long be so! Almost every week I hear preachers and laymen ask questions who have suddenly been thrust by the reality of modern-day demon activity into study and conclusions regarding it. I meet folks almost every week with a why-hasn't-somebody-told-me-this-before whine in their voice about information on the devil and demons. This is precisely why this division of the volume had to be written. If I were in a popularity contest this part would have been omitted! Amen!

A Recommendation

This is not a work on demons; I am an ill-equipped novice in the field. There are some who have made life-long studies in the area, who deserve to be read and heard. Others have made recent contributions in the field which are classics and will serve as milestones for future studies by honest students. Permit me to recommend some of these here. These are just a few among many that are good.

Biblical Demonology and *Demons in the World Today* by Merill F. Unger. These are classics in the field of demonology. The latest book *Demons in the World Today* makes some needed shifts in emphasis in the area of Christians and demon influence. These books are biblically sound and extremely helpful to the beginning student of the subject. They will stand as continuous classics with a scholarly respectability.

The works of Kurt Koch have recently come to the horizon of Christian awareness. Koch is a German scholar who has given his life to study and research in the area of occultism and demonology with both a psychological and spiritual perspective. His research has included travel around the world and thousands of cases of counselling with those oppressed. Here is a list of four of his volumes which have to do with demonology and related subjects: *Christian Counselling and Occultism, Between Christ and Satan, The Devil's Alphabet, Occult Bondage and Deliverance.*

The Bible, the Supernatural and the Jews by McCandlish Phillips has proven to be an honest and helpful volume in a wide area of related subjects to the whole realm of the unseen world. This includes the occult, the devil, demons, angels, deliverance, and such. I have found it to be a delightfully balanced volume.

Christianity and the Occult by J. Stafford Wright is a good volume on the subject, sane and down to earth. He wisely relates many of the phenomena in the world to the teaching of the Bible against the occult.

Demon Experiences in Many Lands is a compilation published by Moody Press. This is a presentation of a number of shocking case studies from all over the world of demon oppression and influence. It corresponds to many reports which continue to flood in from the foreign fields and a growing number of like reports from our very own country!

Demons, Demons, Demons is a recent publication of Broadman Press from the brilliant pen and mind of John Newport, respected professor of Southwestern Baptist Theological Seminary. This is a welcome scholarly work to the field of demonology. It is sane, sensible, open, fair, and satisfying work on the reality of the supernatural in the area of the occult and demons. It will pave the way for many a person to study this area who, because of intellectual hang-ups, would never otherwise have entered in.

Defeated Enemies by Corrie ten Boom is a simple little booklet on victory over the devil and demons from one whose experiences uniquely prepare her for work in this area. I have had the rare privilege of watching this woman deal with cases of demon oppression and can testify to its genuineness.

Space would fail to mention books and booklets which are being published every month now. Dwight Pentecost, in his classic work, *The Devil,* gives a brief space to demon traffic which is helpful. These are only a few of many that I could recommend for your reading.

Demons in the Old Testament

The reality of demons dawns on the consciousness of the Bible reader early. Though demons or spirits of evil are to be found in the Old Testament, they are not dealt with in an orderly fashion. The first reference to spirits other than Satan is made in Genesis 6, where the sons of God came and cohabited with the daughters of men. Some students believe that fallen angels and demon spirits are two classes of beings distinctly separate. The demons are believed to be the unnatural offspring of the "sons of God," the fallen angels, and the daughters of men. This seems to be mere supposition and cannot be an established conclusion.

Psalm 96:4-5 says, "For the Lord is great, and greatly to be praised; he is to be feared above all gods. For all the gods of the nations are idols; but the Lord made the heavens." This seems to indicate that David realized that there were other "gods" or spirit beings besides God. It is likely that just as he taught and believed the existence of good spirits or angels, he taught about evil spirits. There are many times when David makes reference in the Psalms to those who are his enemies when we can suspect that these enemies are more than human. "Plead my cause with them which fight against me . . . and let the angel of the Lord chase them; let their way be dark and slippery; and let the angel of the Lord persecute them" (Ps. 35:1,6). This sounds more like spirit warfare than what men are accustomed to experiencing. I believe that this is a case of demon harassment as are many other references in the Psalms.

In Psalm 106:30-37 we read, "And they served their idols which were a snare to them. Yea, they sacrificed their sons and daughters to devils [demons]." This is an irrefutable case for demons in the Old Testament and clears a picture that has been dark in my mind for a long time. Most of my life I have been puzzled as to why God was so vehement in his intolerance of witchcraft and the like. I have always felt that there was absolutely nothing to the whole picture and discounted it as a total hoax. I have learned that this is not so. Not only are idolatry and witchcraft wrong because they leave off the worship of God, but they open the life to demons as they are literally demon worship.

There is clear evidence in Exodus 7:11 that there was a supernatural power, not of God, which was available to the sorcerers and the magicians of Egypt. Witchcraft was such a severe infraction of the rules of God that He said in Exodus 22:18, "Thou shalt not suffer a witch to live."

In 2 Kings 21:4-6 the record is that Manasseh "built altars for *all the host of heaven* in the house of the Lord. And he made his son to pass through the fire, and observed times, and enchantments, and *dealt with familiar spirits* and wizards [male witches]." The worship of demons was warned against time and again and the practice of it cost great kings their lives and nations their welfare.

Saul is the clearest case of demonization in the Old Testament, and his case can be traced in its developments. In 1 Samuel 15 we read of his partial obedience which is the most subtle form of disobedience—using his own judgment instead of obeying God's command. When he used the cause of God for an excuse, Samuel replied, "Behold, to obey is better than sacrifice, and to hearken than the fat of rams. FOR REBELLION IS AS THE SIN OF WITCHCRAFT, AND STUBBORNNESS IS AS INIQUITY AND IDOLATRY" (1 Sam. 15:22-23).

That disobedience cost Saul his throne, though he kept the position for some time after that. In 1 Samuel 16:14 we read "But the Spirit of the Lord departed from Saul, AND AN EVIL SPIRIT FROM THE LORD TROUBLED HIM." His servants saw it and found that music alleviated the manifestations to some degree. The last verse of 1 Samuel 16 informs us, "David took an harp, and played with his hand; so Saul was refreshed, and was well, and the evil spirit departed from him." Later Saul became jealous over the acclaim that came to David in the slaughter of Goliath, and his sin was compounded. It was obvious that the evil spirit that had departed now returned. Saul became a man obsessed, and his life ended in stark tragedy, a victim of the devil.

Saul finally consulted the witch of Endor and in doing it drew to himself more of the wrath of God. "So Saul died for his transgression which he committed against the Lord, even against the Word of the Lord, which he kept now, and also for asking counsel of one that had a familiar spirit [demon], to inquire of it . . . and inquired not of the Lord" (1 Chron. 10:13-14).

Demons in the New Testament

Even the rankest liberals in the New Testament record believed in the existence of demons. The scribes are recorded in Mark 3 as saying, "He hath Beelzebub, and by the prince of devils casteth out devils." (This word "devils" should be properly translated "demons.") The folks in the synagogue where Jesus encountered His first demon certainly believed in demons. They were amazed, not at the existence of unclean spirits, but at the manner of authority Jesus exerted over them.

Dealing with demons was a vital part of the ministry of Jesus and probably occupied at least one fourth of his ministry. He dealt definitely and decisively with demons and gave his disciples authority to do the same. "Behold, I give unto you power [authority] to tread on serpents and scorpions, and over all the power of the enemy; AND NOTHING SHALL BY ANY MEANS HURT YOU" (Luke 10:18).

Both the presence and prominence of demons is an undeniable fact of the New Testament. We shall deal more with this as we come to discuss the record of demons.

It will suffice to say at this point that victory over the devil will include victory over his demons. Both the devil and his demons are very much with us. We cannot be wise and deny the existence of either. There is nothing recorded that would give us any freedom to believe that demons have ceased to be. I wish there were. But since there is not, we face an unanswerable paradox. If we are people who believe the Book, why have we avoided the face-to-face confrontation necessary to defeat the devil and his demons in the lives of people?

My conviction is that many in the coming seasons will *pulverize* the *paradox* by lining their ministries up with the Bible. There will be a great growth among evangelical Christians in the ministry of delivering the oppressed within the next months. This comes late, but is nevertheless welcome! THE OBVIOUS IS OBVIOUS . . . DEMONS ARE WITH US!

The Occult and Demons

This brief discussion is somewhat parenthetical, but is vitally related to the subject of demons in general. My conviction is that one of the greatest encouragements to demon entrance today is in the area of the occult. The Israelites were warned of the grave dangers of the occult in Deuteronomy 18:9-12. The list given compares with a directory of occult practices which have recently become a part of a massive revival in our nation. Included in this list are. . .

fortune telling,

astrology,

enchanting,

witchcraft,

and consulting the dead. These are simply designated as being AN ABOMINATION UNTO THE LORD.

Kurt Koch's book *The Devil's Alphabet* is a splendid book on the various occult practices of history. The word "occult" is derived from a Latin word "occultus," meaning "hidden, mysterious, or concealed." Though occult practices may accommodate themselves to the culture of the countries in which they are practiced, the underlying principles have remained basically unchanged for thousands of years. The devil may change his face to meet the culture of the time and place, but his purpose is always the same . . . to *steal,*

kill,

and *destroy.*

There is evidence that in the near future there will be a new thrust by all areas involved with the occult, a sort of ecumenical togetherness on the part of the demonic. Ignorance on the part of the Christian will prove costly indeed. Many Christians are involved on the fringes of the occult without any knowledge of the fact that demons are welcomed by the practice of the occult. Many have replied to a warning by saying, "But I never took any of this seriously. I really didn't believe in it!"

This makes about as much sense as taking a bottle of poison and replying after being informed, "Well, I really wasn't serious when I did it!" Innocently or deliberately they will die just as dead. Listen to what the respected scholar, Merrill Unger, says in his latest book, *Demons in the World Today*: "The counseling experience of Dr. Kurt Koch and others has established that occult involvement often results in demonic oppression or subjection that will sometimes affect even the third and fourth generation (Ex. 20:3-5). The family members who become believers can be affected and in need of deliverance even if they have not dealt in the occult. Believers who persist in flagrant sin may be driven by demons into emotional instability, insanity, or even suicide. Severe demon influence can produce enslavement and subjection even if it does stop short of actual possession."

Yes, demons are a reality whether you and I like it or not. (And I don't!) But this is no time for the old ostrich head-in-the-sand trick. Let's face it and find facts that come with facing the issue.

6. The Record of Demons

We will relate in this chapter a brief background of the activity of demons in the New Testament, and cases involving demons in recent days. Again let it be remembered that the reason for entering into this study is not to *satisfy* the curiosity, but to *secure* the victory.

Summary of Demon Influence in the New Testament

There were many types of demonization in the New Testament. It should be mentioned at this juncture that the term "demon possessed" is probably unfortunate. It is a mistranlation of the word meaning to "demonize," which covers many varying degrees of demonic influence or control. The effect of this translation has caused misconceptions as to who may be subjected to demon influence. There are thousands and even millions of people in our world today who have a rather normal life who are under demon control in a part of their lives and will never be free until they are delivered from the demon power.

If a person who has a demon or is demonized, receives a wrong diagnosis, it will result in a wrong treatment and recovery will be impossible.

The most famous case of demonization in the New Testament is the wild man of Gadara. He is the exception instead of the rule. In fact he is the only one of his kind mentioned. (In one case two are mentioned as being present on that occasion.) He was a man truly possessed. He was isolated, living in the tombs, possessed supernatural strength, totally incapacitated to normal living, and lived naked. It would be helpful to compare these tendencies to the rising frequency of demonization today. There are very few people today demonically controlled to this degree who are available for observation. Most of them are institutionalized, and many of them die within a brief period of time.

To the contrary the first recorded demonized man Jesus met was in the synagogue, evidently worshipping along with the rest of the people. When Jesus taught with authority the unclean spirit in the man became aroused and began to speak to Jesus, whereupon Jesus said in effect, "Shut up and get out!" The unclean spirit then cried with a loud voice and left him immediately (Mark 1:23-26).

From then on statements such as these are common:

"And he healed many that were sick of divers diseases and cast out many devils" (Mark 1:34).

"And he preached in their synagogues throughout all Galilee, and cast out devils" (Mark 1:39).

"For he healed many; insomuch that they presed upon him to touch him, as many had plagues. AND UNCLEAN SPIRITS, when they saw him, fell down before him, and cried, Thou art the Son of God (Mark 3:10-11).

It is not out of reason to assume that when Jesus rebuked the sea during the storm recorded in Mark 4, He was talking to an evil spirit behind the foul weather. It is not without note that what He said to the wind and the sea was almost identical to the word to what He said to the demonized man in the synagogue!

Multiplied thousands of people were doubtlessly among those who were delivered by the power of the loving Savior. There must have been cases of mass deliverances. This would lead us to believe that demonization was indeed common in Jesus' day.

49

There was at least one occasion in which Jesus delivered a young girl without even being in her presence. This was the case of the Syrophenician woman's daughter, recorded in Mark 7:25-30. It is of vital interest to note that in this instance the mother's faith was all that was needed for the victory.

Jesus encountered people with demons that affected them physically. In Matthew 17 an epileptic boy is delivered of a demon and is completely cured. In Luke 13 is the record of a woman who had a serious case of spinal curvature. Jesus healed her, informing the people that Satan had bound her these many years. In Matthew 9 a dumb (speechless) man was brought to Jesus. When the demon was cast out, the man was able to speak. All the speech therapy in the world would have been of no avail, but a world from Jesus brought deliverance. These are only a few cases which demonstrate the ability of demons to impose physical hindrances on people. A medical doctor recently approximated that at least 40 percent of the patients that he saw had physical symptoms that were direcly demonic, not to speak of many who had psychosomatic symptoms.

This summary should give us a background which allows us to believe that since demons are very much with us today, some of the same types of cases will frequently manifest themselves. Let us have our eyes open to such and learn to deal with it with propriety under the authority of the Scripture.

Demons Today

With the revival of the occult in America there has been a sharp rise in known cases of demonization. Another reason for this increase is a growing awareness of the presence of demonic spirits and an increasing knowledge of the power of the Christian to deal with them authoritatively. You may read from several sources cases of modern demonization. Among these are *Demon Experiences in Many Lands* by Moody Press, *Demon Possession and Allied Themes* by John L. Nevius, and especially *Between Christ and Satan* by Kurt Koch.

The remainder of this chapter will contain cases of demonization or demon influence which are not in print anywhere as far as I know. I write them down with the belief that these stories will serve as points of reference both to those who may be oppressed and need to be freed and to those who know of cases of oppression and should be used in helping set the captives free. Either the people involved in each case have given permission for the use of the information regarding their circumstances or the stories will be told in such generalities that no one could be identified.

When we began to discuss honestly the biblical approach to this subject, amazing things began to happen. Even when we began the discussion, I was somewhat skeptical regarding the actual dealing with demonized people. A few cases served to make a believer out of me, and today I have no doubt whatever of the frequency of demonization even among Christians.

It should be mentioned here that though Christians cannot be possessed in the full sense of the word, they can be influenced, oppressed, obsessed, depressed, and invaded. In a helpful little booklet, Clifton McElheran divides demon influence into three areas: OPPRESSION—attack from the outside; OBSESSION—invasion of the mind or body by evil forces; POSSESSION—the taking over of the entire person by evil spirits.

I have simply taken necessary details from either written or oral reports of the people involved in the following cases. There is a specific reason for publishing the information on each of these, as they serve to relate to us cases of unique importance.

C. L. Culpepper's First Exposure to Demons

C. L. Culpepper was for many years a missionary to China. During his days on the field there he encountered a unique case of demonization. A man had joined the church and had come under suspicion by some of the leadership as having been involved in Satan worship. A group of the members of the church gathered to discuss the problem without informing the man of their meeting. Despite the fact that he had not been informed of the meeting, he appeared at the meeting angry.

Culpepper recognized the characteristics of demonization. As the man became violent, he came against him in the name of Jesus. A battle ensued which ranged from the man's cowering in the corner to his taking a fire shovel and threatening to take the lives of the people in the house. They continued to pray for him until finally there was achieved some peace and it seemed that the demon had gone. The man was told that he was in danger of the demons coming back if he did not get saved. (It was obvious that when he joined the church, he was not saved.) He refused to believe in Jesus and left the meeting unconverted. It was not very many weeks later that the same man jumped in a well, an apparent suicide.

A Demon of Hate

Mrs. A. came to my office and straight forward admitted that she had a spirit of hate for her father. She recognized that it was not her choice to have hate for him, but it was complusive. She further reported that her father had been dead for several years. Further discussion revealed that on an occasion that she could remember her father told her about a gypsie woman who had told him she was putting a curse on him. He admitted all the rest of his life that it seemed to him that his life was cursed. We remarked that it was possible that the curse may have been imposed in reality on her father and passed on to her at his death. (I believe that thousands in our world today are under such curses.)

We prayed that this curse might be broken and that she might be freed from this spirit of hate. I knew so very little about procedure in such matters, but the Lord seemed to accommodate His power to our stage of learning. As I was praying and claiming deliverance for her, I heard a delightful declaration from this woman. "I'm free!" she exclaimed. And indeed she was! She testifies that her whole inner attitude changed immediately, and the feelings of hate for her father have not recurred.

A Demon of Homosexuality

Mr. B. came to me admitting his problem to be one of homosexuality and manifested a deep desire to be delivered, believing it to be demonic in nature. (I am deeply convicted that cases of sexual deviation, as well as many cases of lust or overdesire are directly demonic and can be cured in no other manner than deliverance.) We began dealing with this young man and almost immediately the spirit from within him began to speak to me in a female voice and then threw him on the floor. This was followed by writhings and groanings with the young man in a state of semiconsciousness. It was out of the question that this might be a case of dramatics. The demon was commanded in Jesus' name to come out of him.

A voice came again saying, "I am going, but he is going with me!" At this time without warning the young man jumped up and lunged toward the window. He would have surely gone through the window if we had not grabbed and subdued him physically. The window was broken, and a potted flower was knocked off the windowsill and broken. He began to eat the dirt from the broken flower pot. The name of Jesus was repeated with the command that he be freed until finally he was relaxed in calm repose, completely free.

We learned many things from this case, including the fact that the spirits can be bound from doing harm to the physical body by pleading the blood of Jesus in protection. The young man has remained free and delightedly serves the Savior.

A Demon Visualized

A rare case was reported to me by a woman whose word I have no reason to question. She reported a long history of involvement in various forms of the occult, including membership in a foundation known for occult practices. Recently she was moved to begin to seek the Lord in total commitment. She decided to fast and pray for several days. As this fast was in its early stages the desire for the Lord increased and with that desire a sense of unprecedented struggle. The turmoil continued until after many hours she lay face down on her bed, exhausted. As she continued to pray, she felt a strange sensation in her body. Her body seemed to be turning inside out. There was a pulling sensation from the top of the head, from the fingers, and the toes and feet. All the pulling seemed to be toward a spot on her back. She thought that this surely must be death, and yet she remained conscious.

She then felt this force brace itself against her body on the inside as the pulling increased in the area of the upper back. Suddenly with a whooshing sound the thing was released from her body with a sensation of fiery heat being released from her body. She felt like an empty sack, weak, but conscious. She found her head beginning to turn without knowing the reason or being able to stop it.

As she raised her eyes she saw squatted on the corner of an antique table the most horrible creature she could ever have imagined. She described it as being not very big, wet, soggy, filthy, seemingly dripping poison. In this terrifying instant she ran the gamut of emotions including doubting God and His love. As she experienced this doubt, the thing she had seen jumped on her back again. Terrified and hysterical she screamed, "Lord, I didn't mean it! Let me die, but please take this thing off my back. Don't let it get back inside me!" She says, "The Lord heard me. Very gently the thing was lifted from my body . . . it seemed to be dead and nonresistant. I never saw it again."

This was followed by nausea and vomiting and a feeling of complete hollowness. With the relief from the evil spirit, there was no accompanying joy from the Lord. She became afraid that the case of the demon leaving the man and later returning with seven others worse, might be repeated in her case.

She called me at this time because of the suggestion of a friend and we prayed on the phone after she had confessed every occult involvement and claimed forgiveness, taking back all the ground she had ever given the devil. (It might be added here that one involvement she had to confess was membership in a group which studied after Edgar Cayce). She then vowed to rid her home of any occult-related books and objects so as not to give the devil any place. She claimed the fulness of the Holy Spirit and entered into great joy. She has remained delightfully free and serves as one of our loyal prayer intercessors.

Oppression from Occult Studies

Mrs. C reports, "My experience with the study of the occult started in a rather sophisticated way—a college course in psychology. The first introduction to parapsychology, as it was called, came under the topic of the human mind. Some of the subtopics presented were ESP, mental telepathy, dream interpretation, reincarnation, out-of-body travel, thought transference, mind reading, handwriting analysis, calling up spirits, the religion of spiritism, mediums, and other topics dealing with psychic phenomena.

"Films were shown and topics discussed on both positive and negative mental control. Other phases of the occult were discussed with an attitude of fun and excitement. The instructor told of his study and experiments in the field and related experiences in audience with fortune-tellers, mediums, and interpreters of dreams.

"Assignments both required and optional were made to hear Jeane Dixon lecture and give predictions, attend lectures on Edgar Cayce's psychic phenomena, visit fortune-tellers and mediums, and read books covering all phases of parapsychology."

Mrs. C reported further that the instructor seemed to single her out with a few others and encouraged them to pursue this area. After much persuading, she decided that she and her husband would go to a fortune-teller, just to prove that there wasn't anything to it. The woman with whom they had audience began to share facts that she had no way of knowing such as a serious illness from which Mr. C almost died. She correctly identified the kind of illness he suffered. She correctly identified the number and sex of their children, giving specific incidents in their lives and their personality traits. She related that she saw a dream that he had dreamed over and over again. He could not remember one.

The next day Mrs. C made an anonymous appointment with the same medium. She became aware during this visit that the medium indeed did have powers that were tapping her mind. She correctly pointed out a stomach disorder. Emotional upset followed this visit to the point that Mrs. C thought that she was going crazy. (She is a very stable woman emotionally.) She began to pray and search the Scriptures as never before. A period of mental confusion and frustration followed in which she says, "It seemed like I was watching a tug-of-war from a front-row box seat, only it seemed that my mind, not a rope, was being used." She made a wilful choice in the midst of all this to refuse all relationships with the occult. She burned books, papers, and research notes on the subjects. We visited together and resisted the devil and all related spirits. She is free now and much the wiser and more cautious!

Demonized Man Invades Home of Intercessor

In the latter part of 1971 an evangelist friend of mine, Jim Hylton, some others, and I were praying one morning after the midnight hour at the church. All of sudden Jim stood up and began to resist the devil very vociferously. I wondered why he was doing this, as I did not feel any special oppression in the prayer time. After the prayer Jim remarked that he did not know why, but he was compelled to stand against the devil and felt that surely he was attacking someone who needed that prayer of resistance.

The next day we learned that at that same time that we were praying the night before a man had broken into the home of one of our most ardent intercessors and attacked members of the family. In the attack the husband was stabbed, but not hurt seriously. After as long as fifteen minutes of struggle the woman came to herself and recognized that this was of the devil. Up to this point nothing had worked to discourage the young man.

He continued to fight and refused to leave. Finally she took her authority position and said to him, "In the name of Jesus Christ, I demand you to leave this house." He immediately responded, gathered up items he had dropped from his pockets in the scuffle and took his leave. It should be remembered that the crisis occurred just at the time that Jim had felt compelled to stand up and resist the devil.

There have been many others and there will be many more. At this point the reader will have experienced rather drastic reaction if there is any reaction within. If it will help, I might right now declare that for me this is no fad or tangent, but an area of study and ministry into which I have been drawn by the Spirit of God. Had I the slightest doubt of this leadership this volume would never have been born. Before you make judgments or even severe assumptions, please declare your heart open to the teaching ministry of the Holy Spirit. God may well desire to use you to LET THE OPPRESSED GO FREE.

7. The Recognition and Removal of Demons

This is a vital chapter to victory over the devil. It makes little difference how much we know about the enemy and his agents, if we do not know how to recognize and remove them. We can learn much just by watching Christ in action in the New Testament. We have the right to use His name. All that He did in the power of God is available to us in the use of His name. In His name we can know what we cannot know in ourselves. In His name we can do what we could never do in ourselves. In His name we have authority that we do not have in ourselves. BLESS HIS NAME! At that name the devil must come to attention and the demons must obey.

There are many cases in which we can be safe in assuming the need of deliverance without knowing of the existence of manifestations. Any involvement in the occult is an open invitation for demon entrance. A few of these are listed to give the reader an idea of areas where grave dangers lie. I have found an appalling ignorance across the land regarding these areas even among Christians.

Astrology.—This is expressingly and repeatedly forbidden in Scripture because it involves consulting other sources than God for information. In the case of the demon visualized in the preceding chapter the woman was deeply involved for a long period of time in astrology. When the Lord delivered her, she was a believer indeed that the demons loved to connect themselves to someone thus interested in the occult. She is now so definite about avoiding any contact with it that she cuts the section on horoscopes out of her newspaper and throws it away before she takes the paper in the house.

Cartomancy.—This is a means of foretelling the future through card laying. This appeals greatly to the curious nature of people and seems innocent enough. With a pack of playing cards there are thousands of combinations forecasting the future. This art is widely practiced and perhaps the most famous user of this method is Jeane Dixon.

Psychometry.—This is the art of holding an article belonging to someone not present and describing that person through the knowledge given supernaturally. Many clairvoyants will display this power publicly by asking folks in the audience to turn in articles and describing their owners correctly. This power is supernatural, but not from God.

Magic.—True magic is relying on the supernatural for things desired. There is much magic today which is simple slight of hand, but it is derived and thus still related to the godless magic powers we read about in Egypt. The Bible is very candid in describing the power of the Egyptian magicians in their contest with Moses and Aaron. It was not that they did not have super-natural powers, but in the final analysis the power of God was greater than the power of the devil.

Amulets.—An amulet is something worn for good luck. This simply amounts to a compensation for a lack of faith in God. Even the age-old custom of a team's having a mascot is derived from ancient times when these were trusted in for aid from supernatural means.

Reading occult literature.—The devil takes advantage of the natural tendencies of men. Man has an insatiable appetite for the unknown. Anything strange appeals to most of us. Occult bookstores are cropping up all across America. Recently an entire set of occult encyclopedias were offered through the mail with a beautiful multicolor brochure depicting these books in almost life size. The occult in the mails is continuing to grow at an alarming rate. I have not been able to even use occult material in research without problems. The Christian should rid his home and office of such material including objects and trinkets imported from lands where demonization is rampant if they be demonic in background.

Palmistry.—This art is perhaps more commonly practiced by most forms of the occult. It is simply put, the art of reading palms. Palmistry can be traced back to ancient Rome and per-haps farther back than that. The palm is supposed to have the four main lines, head, heart, fate, and life. It is divided into seven planet mounds thus making interesting the art of palm reading. A friend of mine, a committed Christian, practiced palm reading as a pasttime and as party entertainment. It always made for good conversation. After study in the field of the occult and its inherent dangers, he renounced it and was delivered.

Divining rod and pendulum.—This is used for anything from finding underground water to discovering oil. I find folks who are shocked that the old method of water witching is occult in nature, not scientific. A pendulum practitioner with a map and a pendulum can find lost objects or people and discover oil.

Witchcraft.—The practice of witchcraft in one form or another is experiencing one of the greatest revivals in history. The Middle Ages seems to have come alive in our very midst. There are many forms of witchcraft which include communication with the dead, calling up the devil, incantations, the use of certain herbs for magical purposes, and the casting of spells. It has its own Bible, *The Book of Shadows,* and is characterized by a misuse of biblical terms and concepts. Its supreme characteristic includes the concept of the union between Christ and Satan. We have experienced in recent days the deliverance of several from the craft. There will be more!

Yoga.—Some of the most prominent people practice yoga as a physical exercise system which seems to be beneficial to health. I used to believe that it was harmless. One experience made a believer out of me in its harmfulness. A couple came to me years ago for some advice regarding a business they planned to begin. They were planning to open a yoga club and asked me if there was anything about this which would run counter to their Christian profession. Had I known then what I know now, I would vigorously warned against it and advise thusly. They related that they did not intend to get into the religion of yoga, but were going to use the system of bodily exercises and positions. I HAVE FOUND SINCE THAT IT IS NOT POSSIBLE TO TAKE A PART OF THE DEVIL'S PROGRAM AND LEAVE THE REST. The business eventually folded, but they were in it long enough to be drawn away from their loyalty to Christ. They need deliverance wherever they are today.

Eastern Religions.—There is a spread of Buddhism and Islam in our nation today. Many folks deem that this is an eventuality stemming from youthful rebellion. It is nothing short of a demonic invasion, and to dabble in Eastern religion or Eastern mysticism is purely occult and deadly dangerous.

We could go on and on with dozens of practices that are being introduced into American life today. It has even been suggested that the art of acupuncture is derived from an ancient practice of the use of needles in witchcraft. A form of this is practiced in certain primitive areas of the world today. In Kurt Koch's book

60

on *Revival in Indonesia* the practice of such is mentioned on the Island of Timor.

These have been mentioned not only as a warning, but as a suggestion that anyone engaging in them may be in need of deliverance.

Conditions Which May Suggest Demonization

Continued compulsions.—Not every compulsion is a demon, but many of them are. I am convinced that many of the problems we are trying to deal with as far as habits are concerned could be easily dealt with if the cause, a demon, was removed. The devil takes advantage of the human frame which tends toward habit and builds strongholds for his demons. The compulsion may never be broken until the personality behind it is broken. This may involve such things as smoking, drinking, overeating, talking, working, or spending.

Chronic fears.—Fear is one of the commonest of demon powers. There are dozens of phobias which oppress Christians and some of the most victorious Christians I have known have areas of needless fears. They may have derived from an experience a long time ago, but that influence can be broken. There are such fears as close places, high places, water, crowds, routines, storms, and death. A fear which is unreasoning is apt to have behind it a demon power.

Unnatural sex desires.—I have little doubt that behind cases of unnatural sex there are demon powers. These are some of the strongest demons the devil has. Where there is spiritual revival there will appear on the scene inevitably people with these problems. I have seen homosexuals, lesbians, and others involved in sexual deviation delivered completely.

Mental suffering.—Worry is a habit which may lead to a satanic stronghold. Generally the worrier in this state can find no reason that is consistent to worry. They are worried about worry. Worry breeds more worry, and they find themseves in a veritable prison of worry. It may involve guilt, shame, inferiority feelings, or any combination of mental torments.

61

Involuntary feelings and actions.—A continued feeling of unreasoned hate should be investigated quickly. Actions involving a burst of temper should be suspicioned as being demonic. When I hear someone say, "I don't know what made me do that!" I begin to suspicion the power of a demon. When there is continued and helpless self-consciousness, depression, or unexplainable tendencies toward excess we should be on guard.

Wierd unbiblical beliefs.—Paul warned that in the latter days "Many shall depart from the faith, giving heed to SEDUCING SPIRITS, AND DOCTRINES OF DEMONS" (1 Tim. 4:1). This refers to doctrines propogated by actual evil spirits. There have never been as many wierd beliefs as are floating around today. I feel every now and then as if I have heard everything, and then something else more ridiculous than ever will come along. When I witness these beliefs which did not come from the Word of God, I can be certain someone has been listening to and believing evil spirits.

Destructive dreams.—I have had the experience of staying in a motel room and being harassed by dreams of such nature that I would not even tell my nearest friends about. They do not fit into the ordinary pattern of dreams. Things that my mind has never before entertained came invading my mind through the dream. Matters came across my consciousness that I would never have wilfully given entrance. I dealt with it as a demonic force and the dreams did not recur. I believe that many dreams are demonically caused and sometimes deliverance is the only cure.

An inordinate desire for attention.—The lack of love in a person's past may lead them to desire to feel wanted so much that they strive for attention in strange ways. Demons are ready to pick up on a need like this until varied forms of striving for attention appear, including the grossest forms of exhibitionism and dramatics.

Physical symptoms unexplained.—A boy had an evil spirit of epilepsy and was delivered by Jesus. A woman was almost bent over double and had a spirit of infirmity cast out of her. A man had a deaf, dumb, and blind spirit and was cured when the demon was gone. I am convinced that many physical symptoms that have been unyielding are demon powers which have attached themselves to people. There is a clear relationship in the New Testament between diseases and demons and this should be recognized as a possibility today.

Sometimes the look in the eyes or the countenance of the face can be a tell-tale sign of the presence of demon powers. Physical affectations may reveal inner frustrations brought about by demonic powers.

Alcohol and Drug Addiction

There is little doubt in my mind that in virtually every case of alcoholism and drug addiction demons are involved. Generally there are several which group together around these conditions. Demons love company. When one is weakened to the state of the alcoholic or the drug addict, many unclean spirits will join together in taking up their abode in that person.

Thus, it is necessary to consider that in any cure that is going to be of permanent nature, demons must be considered. This is a hard pill to swallow in our sophisticated culture where these abnormalities are looked upon as only serious social illnesses. We are discovering, however, that these people are generally not cured until the stronghold of the devil is pulled down in their lives and the demon powers behind the compulsions are removed by the power of God. Alcohol and drugs are two open doors to the demon world and each as serious as the other.

There are many other conditions which could be mentioned. Let there be issued here a warning that we have not said that everyone who suffers from any one of these has a demon. I have said that these are some of the symptoms which *may* reveal the presence of the demonic. If a whole book was written about the total symptomatic spectrum, it would not be sufficient to preclude the need for SPIRITUAL DISCERNMENT. Without discernment we are in dangerous territory and it would be well to tarry until we be endued!

At this point research material dwindles down to a mere trickle. I now have no more than a few booklets, tracts, and pamphlets to which to refer for resource material on the subject of deliverance. This looks like the trend. . . .

much on the devil,

less on demons,

still less on actual demon influence today,

almost nothing on what to do about it in a practical way.

I do have the Bible and a great deal of practical material in the pages of the New Testament where I find Jesus facing the distressed, obsessed, possessed, and depressed and doing something decisive about it. I cannot believe that He would have you and me do anything less than stand against these forces in the authority of His blood, the power of His name, and the force of His Word.

There are a few people today who are becoming known around the nation for their work in the area of deliverance from demon powers. They are kept so busy that in most cases there are waiting lists for months to come. They are ridiculed, criticized, villified, and attacked by many Christians, some well-intentioned. However, I like the way they are doing it better than the way we are not! I cannot believe it pleasing to God for you and me to have to walk away from seeming impossible cases of demonic oppression and slavery without an answer.

IF THE SPIRIT OF THE LORD GOD IS UPON ME . . . THEN I HAVE THE AUTHORITY TO PROCLAIM LIBERTY TO THE CAPTIVES JUST AS JESUS DID, BECAUSE HE WHO SAID IT IS IN ME! There are hundreds of thousands who are captive, brokenhearted, crushed by circumstances, and bruised by depression who need to be freed. Jesus has promised freedom. He both secures it and sustains it. Praise the Lord!

Suggestions for Preparation

Recognize authority completely—We have discussed this before, but be reminded that the devil was stripped of his authority and all authority was given to Jesus (Matt. 28:18). It is well to assert the passages in 1 John 4:17 "BECAUSE AS HE IS, SO ARE WE IN THIS WORLD." Is He sufficient? Then so are we IN HIM! Does He have power and authority over demons? Then so do we IN HIM! Will they obey His commands? Then so they must obey ours IN HIM!

Wield the Word Effectively.—We have discovered that the reading of the Word is powerful to give confidence and prepare the heart for the work of the Spirit in deliverance. It causes the faith to rise within a person's heart. Such verses as the following have proven to be of maximum effectiveness in heart preparation for both the one to be delivered and the one being used by the Lord in deliverance.

> 2 Corinthians 10:4-5—"For the weapons of our warfare are not carnal, but mighty through God to the pulling down of strongholds; casting down imaginations, and every high thing that exalteth itself against the knowledge of God, and bringing into captivity every thought to the obedience of Christ."

> Luke 10:17-18—"And the seventy returned again with joy, saying, Lord, even the devils [demons] are subject unto us through thy name. And He said unto them, Behold, I give unto you power to tread on serpents and scorpions, and over all power of the enemy and nothing shall by any means hurt you."

> 1 John 4:4—"Ye are of God, little children, and have overcome them [any spirit confessing not Christ's coming in the flesh]; because greater is he that is in you than he that is in the world."

> 1 John 5:4—"For whatsoever is born of God overcometh the world; and this is the victory that overcometh the world, even our faith."

> Matthew 12:28—"If I cast out demons by the Spirit of God, then the kingdom of God is come unto you."

> 1 John 1:7—"But if we walk in the light as he is in the

light we have fellowship one with another and the blood of Jesus Christ, his Son, cleanseth us from all sin."

Hebrews 2:14-15—". . . that through death he might destroy him who had the power of death, that is, the devil, And DELIVER them who through fear of death were all their lifetime subject to bondage."

2 Corinthians 2:14—"But thanks be to God, which always causeth us to triumph in Christ, and maketh manifest the savour of his knowledge by us in every place."

Joel 2:32—"And it shall come to pass, that whosoever shall call upon the name of the Lord shall be delivered."

Philippians 4:31—"I can do all things through Christ which strengtheneth me."

Isaiah 59:19—"So shall they fear the name of the Lord from the West, and his glory from the rising of the sun. WHEN THE ENEMY SHALL COME IN LIKE A FLOOD, THE SPIRIT OF THE LORD SHALL LIFT UP A STANDARD AGAINST HIM."

Isaiah 54:17—"No weapon that is formed against thee shall prosper; and every tongue that shall rise against thee in judgment, thou shalt condemn."

Jeremiah 1:19—"And that shall fight against thee; but they shall not prevail against thee; FOR I AM WITH THEE, SAITH THE LORD, TO DELIVER.

Continuous reading of the Word of God will bring Scriptures to our attention that can be effectively used against the devil. It is extremely important to memorize the Word. The demons believe the Word as does the devil and they have no recourse under the authority of the Word.

Plead the blood constantly.—We have spoken elsewhere of the power of the blood of Christ, and I cannot stress its importance too much. I believe that the devil and every demon was a witness to the cross. Had they known all the truth they would never have perpetrated the foul deed, for it was their doing. It is through the blood that they were defeated and will be finally crushed. The sight or thought of the blood of Jesus

66

is a vital tool in the ministry of deliverance. Again, I repeat, it represents all that Jesus did in our behalf and makes it immediately available to us. I do not fail to reckon the power of the blood over my home, friends, church, possessions, family, and my own physical body. The concept of the blood of Jesus forms a barrier which hell cannot break through. The application of the implications of the blood makes conditions intolerable for demon powers. We need to learn to pray according to our privileges in the Scripture.

> "Father, in Jesus' name, I praise You and I have been delivered from the powers of darkness and have been translated into the Kingdom of Your Son. I thank You that in Him I have died and in Him I now live. I thank You that as He is, so am I in the world. I claim all that He is now through me for this ministry. I now agree with Calvary's victory and now by faith update that victory through this very moment and this situation. Thank You Lord for NOW victory! Pleading the blood and all He did I claim deliverance in Jesus' Name . . . AMEN AND AMEN!"

Use the name repeatedly.—The devil knows that name . . . the name of Jesus! He knows, respects, fears, and trembles. That name cannot be used too much. He has given us unlimited right to wield that name. It is through His name that He enters into the situation with all His power and does the task.

Steps in Procedure

After acquainting one with the authority, the Word, the blood, and the name, it is helpful to consider several suggestions. No method should be unflexible. Many times the case will set the method. In other cases there will be simple discernment moment by moment, which shuns all methods.

1. A formal declaration of desire and intention. When the subject needing deliverance hears himself say, "I believe that Jesus Christ is the Son of God and my Savior. I believe that my inheritance included deliverance over the powers of darkness and I now state my declaration, desire, and intention to be free in

Jesus' name," he takes a positive step toward freedom.

2. A confession of every sin of every kind with a renunciation of every bit of ground ever given through the devil. We are informed in 1 Samuel 15:23 that "rebellion is as the sin of witchcraft, and stubbornness is as iniquity and idolatry." A prayer such as this is in order:

> Father, in Jesus name, I confess the sin of (name specific sins and instances) and renounce it, refuse it, and reject it. I close every door I have ever opened to the devil through any occult practice of (name specific involvements). I now take back any ground I have ever given to the devil and give it to Jesus. I am a child of God and choose for my life the Lordship of Christ and the fulness of the Holy Spirit. I agree with _____ that Jesus can deliver me and commit myself to claim and receive that deliverance now.

3. A coming against the demon powers in the name of Jesus, speaking directly to them and demanding that they come out in that name. It is here that there is a wide divergence in methods and practices. Some have the demons to speak to them, giving them their names. I can testify from experience that demons can use the vocal chords of their subjects and reply. There are others who insist that there is no reason to give the demons such a right.

Some in this ministry demand certain physical manifestations such as convulsions, cryings out, coughing, and vomiting. I can also testify that I have seen this happen with valid and lasting results. It is at this point that certain warnings should be issued:

(1.) If you demand information from the demon, remember that he is a liar and cannot be trusted.

(2.) Don't predict in your mind certain manifestations, refusing to accept deliverance unless they come.

(3.) Don't play games with the demon. If you expect a battle the demons will give you one!

(4.) Don't argue with the demon. You are right in the Word of God, and authority does not need to argue! We recently dealt with a girl that was one of the most severe cases I have witnessed.

I greatly feared that if she was not delivered, she would soon be dead. She was gloriously delivered, but not until after she became hostile even though she had driven a long way to see us. She wanted to accuse and argue and call us names. There was no use of our entering into an argument. I have made that mistake before.

After writing the main body of this chapter I have been involved in different types of deliverance ministries with those who have had much experience in this area. The type of ministry that I have observed to be most effective is that which involves the gift of discernment of spirits and the demand for their dismissal on the basis of that discernment. This is not to depreciate any other kind of approach, but simply to designate the one observed to be most immediate in its results. There will be as many approaches as there are soul-winning techniques.

"RESIST THE DEVIL AND HE SHALL FLEE FROM YOU," is the multiple COMMAND and PROMISE OF James 4:7. We must stand on that and hold it up before the demon powers until they are subdued and dismissed. This is the beginning of freedom. The next chapter will enter an area on which little has been written, but much is needed. Read on!

8. Rules for Remaining Free

Are you still reading? Don't quit now! We now come to some material which is vital, but not found in print in any great quantity. Because so many have a cultural problem in dealing with demons as well as traditional problems, most never get to this point, namely the problem of postdeliverance care. As the new-born soul into the kingdom of God demands care, so does the soul that has been delivered from the snare of the devil. The days immediately following deliverance are vital days, and much care is needed. Let us suggest some areas of continued help.

Helpful Hints to Remember

Immediate deliverance does not suggest immediate normalcy. A person may be completely and instantaneously delivered from the presence of a demon and continue to suffer some "hangover" effects in his life. This may occur physically, mentally, or spiritually, or all three for that matter. A person may quite smoking, but it will generally be days before his system works out all the results of the habit. He has immediately quit, but he is not immediately normal or free from all the effects of the habit of smoking.

The dismissal of a demon does not mean that the devil or demons will be unable to communicate from then on. That same person may be harrassed from the outside by the foul spirits. He should simply be taught that . . .

THE DEMONS TREMBLE WHEN THEY SEE THE WEAKEST OF SAINTS BEND A KNEE! ! ! !

Thus, when the powers of darkness behold the new-found confidence and strength in prayer on the part of their former subject, they will be discouraged from seeking entrance again.

So in summary, let us say that the one set free should be patient, refuse any word that is not from Christ, and should remain in the disposition of prayer.

Helpful Rules to Heed

More than any other people, those delivered from demonization should pay attention to some simple rules such as the following:

Keep short sin accounts!—The moment sin enters, confess it. Let it not linger or else the demons will recognize it as an open invitation to renew their residence. Confess sin the moment conviction dawns. Demons need only a few seconds or a few inches to enter and stand.

Avoid the very appearance of evil!—While this is very good advice, overall it is indispensable advice to those who once have been oppressed by demon powers. Especially to be avoided are those areas which were open doors to the demons in the first place.

In the event of the occult having been the open door, all areas of the occult should be avoided like the plague! If anger has been the open door, fiery outbursts of temper are to be shunned and the power of God sought as the source of calming the tempestous temper.

Walk in the Spirit!—One could become weary of watchfulness here. We are not to live watching for demons. We are to walk in the Spirit and thus give them no room! So often our emphasis is on refraining from evil things, so that we will be righteous. Paul's approach is the opposite . . . WALK IN THE SPIRIT AND YE SHALL NOT FULFILL THE LUSTS OF THE FLESH" (Gal. 5:16). This walk in the Spirit involves being led of the Spirit (Gal. 5:18) and living in the Spirit (Gal. 5:25).

Think freedom!—Paul said, "Stand fast therefore in the liberty wherewith Christ hath made us free, and be not again entangled with the yoke of bondage" (Gal. 5:1). Do not stop at thinking freedom . . . SPEAK FREEDOM. You will have what you say. If you begin to think and speak bondage, you will soon be in bondage again. As we continue to think freedom and confess freedom, it will continue to be a reality. "Seeing then that we have a great High Priest, that is passed into the heaven, Jesus the Son of God, LET US HOLD FAST OUR PROFESSION" (Heb. 4:14). This simply means that we are to continue to confess the reality of our state of deliverance so that our High Priest can keep it before the Father in fresh reality.

Helpful Exercises to Repeat

The exercise of praise is indispensable. We should have learned by now that we are to "praise the Lord at all times" as the psalmist declared (Ps. 34:1). It is an exercise that both encourages the soul and releases the power of God. Aside from this the practice of praise is the worst sound the devil can imagine.

The exercise of witnessing is likewise helpful. The more one repeats what he knows, the better he knows it himself. The witness is most often the happiest because he has just heard himself say what he needs most to believe all the time. If he forgets these verities of the gospel, they may tend to be forgotten. This witnessing can be to the lost, the saved, to one's self, to God, or to the devil. Thus, there is never a time or place when we cannot witness. Try repeating a witness like this when the devil comes around!

"I PRAISE THE LORD THAT JESUS IS MY MIGHTY DELIVERER, AND THAT THROUGH HIM I HAVE BEEN SET FREE. I NOW TESTIFY THAT HE WHO SET ME FREE IS FULLY ABLE TO SUSTAIN MY FREEDOM. I TRUST HIM NOW TO DO THAT!"

Recount your testimony of salvation and deliverance often, even if there is nobody around, but yourself. You will always need to hear it again and certainly the telling of it will freshen its reality.

The exercise of quoting Scripture is a terrible handicap to the devil and his demons. They know all too well that every word in the Book is true. They would very much like to forget it, and that is much the more reason why we should see to it that they will not forget it! When quoting the scripture it is helpful to revise it into testimony form. For instance, take Colossians 1:13 and make it to say, "I HAVE BEEN DELIVERED FROM THE POWERS OF DARKNESS AND HAVE BEEN TRANSLATED INTO THE KINGDOM OF JESUS." The Scripture is our Bill of Rights, and we should quote it in the presence of the principalities and powers in the heavenlies. Aside from quoting the Scripture for the hearing of evil powers, we should repeat it in the hearing of our High Priest, Jesus Christ. As we quote the Scripture re-asserting our agreement with it, our High Priest validates it at the throne and makes it real by the power of His Spirit in terms of reality all around us. Praise the Lord!

The exercise of submission and resistance should be the order of the day for every Christian, but especially the one delivered from demonization. "Submit yourselves therefore to God. Resist the devil and he will flee from you" (James 4:7). This is the _balanced battle,_ on the one hand SUBMISSIVE TO GOD and on the other RESISTING THE DEVIL. This is not a one-time experience, but a continued stance.

Helpful Disciplines to Continue

The discipline of prayer is an absolute necessity. There should be a constant spirit of prayerfulness, but there should also be a set discipline of prayer every day when nothing else occupies the time but conversing with God. HE WHO DOES NOT OFTEN PRAY WILL NOT LONG BE FREE! The devil feels welcome to a prayerless life and often finds easy entrance for his demons. Prayer is the lifeline of continued freedom, the line of defense that guards the positions against the enemy.

The discipline of availability extends the joy of one's deliverance. Often those who have been delivered will be those most used in the ministry of deliverance. Each time another is set free, the joy of former deliverance will be even more vital. He has learned that had it not been for someone's availability, he might not have been freed. Thus, it is his joy to be available to God and to whomever God chooses to be available through him.

The discipline of trials will inevitably come. God will permit these to increase faith, to teach obedience, and to facilitate victory. We are reminded that "Though he were a Son, yet learned he obedience by the things he suffered" (Heb. 5:8). It is often that one can learn more in a few minutes of despair than in days of delight. And besides this, God will not allow us to be tempted past what we can endure (1 Cor. 10:13).

The discipline of implicit trust crowns all the other disciplines. Isaiah reminds us to "TRUST IN THE LORD FOREVER: for in the Lord Jehovah is our strength" (Isa. 26:3-4). "BEHOLD, GOD IS MY SALVATION: I WILL TRUST AND NOT BE AFRAID: FOR THE LORD JEHOVAH IS MY STRENGTH AND MY SONG: HE ALSO IS BECOME MY SALVATION." (Isa. 12:2).

Victory in any field of battle is a team matter. It is not won or kept without the cooperation of a great many soldiers. Likewise, victory over the devil and demons is accomplished by several and sustained by the continued cooperation of God's children. The subject delivered must be made a welcomed member of the fellowship. He should be treated thoughtfully and tenderly with much care being practiced.

The victory is ours! It was appropriated as we stood with one another in the authority of Jesus' name. Let us hold it as we declare together His power to keep us free!

Postscript to Recognition and Removal of Demons: Three Sources of Oppression in the Human Life

The Oppression of a Curse

That curses can be placed on men is without argument. The Bible says that with the tongue we can curse men (James 3:9). The world was made by the Word of God (Heb. 1:3). He created man with the capacity to use words, and those words are powerful for working good and evil. One day as Jesus walked by a fig tree, He found no fruit on it. He put a curse on it, and the next day it was dried up from the roots. Jesus used this experience to teach about the power of the spoken word of faith as He said, "For verily I say unto you, that whosoever shall *say* to this mountain, Be thou removed, and be thou cast into the sea; and shall come to pass; HE SHALL HAVE WHATSOEVER *HE SAITH*." Just as man can bless with his spoken words, he can curse with the same.

For many years I have relegated curses to childplay or pagan imagination. I am now convinced that people by the thousands are walking around with a part of their lives under curses placed upon them by parents, friends, or enemies. Many of these curses are placed by people without intention. Words are the means of curses being placed. We hinder and limit with words. The one victimized by these words may never know that they were said. The enemy, the devil, picks up on our words and makes accusations with them. He accuses God and man, and builds out of those words poisons with which he incarcerates his victims. Jesus tells, "But I say unto you, that every idle word that men shall speak, they shall give account of in the day of judgment. For by thy words thou shalt be justified, and by thy words thou shalt be condemned."

Why are words that important? Simply because they are tools in the hand of the Savior or tools in the hand of the enemy. Words are our confessions. Negative confessions are empowered by the devil and used against God and His children. Positive confessions are employed by the Savior to our good and God's glory. He is the HIGH PRIEST of our profession (Heb. 3:1). When we say it in accord with His will as revealed in His Word, He confesses it as our High Priest before the Father and all of heaven's power is thrown into making it a blessed reality.

The devil is eager to have our bad professions because he can use them against us. If we confess weakness, we are weak. If we confess illness, we are sick. If we confess fatigue, we are tired. If we talk bitterness, we have bitterness, and so on. Criticism, ridicule, hateful words, bitterness are the stuff out of which curses are constructed.

How can you tell when there is a curse in effect? The only answer I know is spiritual discernment. I believe that the gift of discernment includes matters such as this.

What should be done when we encounter a curse? The answer is simple: *RECOGNIZE* it. Mere suspicion is not enough. You can walk around it and call it a dozen other things, but until you have faced it honestly there will be no dealing with it. *REFUTE* it. The curse remains because for years the one upon whom it rests has agreed with it. He has given in to it. It has become a part of his life. We recently dealt with a deeply disturbed woman upon whom there was a curse from a grandmother who practiced psychic powers. Curses can be placed by fortune-tellers or palm readers or the like. These must be refuted! In the name of Jesus and the power of His blood refute the curse. Finally, having refuted it, formally *REJECT* it. That curse cannot stand before the power of the Christ. Choose against every facet of the curse and every result of it and every condition it has brought to pass.

The Oppression of a Demon

We have already dealt with this oppression. I do want this paragraph to appear here in comparison with the oppression of the curse. One may be under a curse without having demon traffic. A curse gives the devil a reason or legal right to harass, but not to possess. In the event of a *curse* it should be *broken*. In the event of a *demon* it should be *expelled*.

The Oppression of a Stronghold

"For the weapons of our warfare are not carnal, but mighty through God to the pulling down of strongholds; casting down imaginations and every high thing that exalteth itself against the knowledge of God and bringing into captivity every thought to the obedience of Christ" (2 Cor. 10:4-5). A stronghold is a set of conditions which a demon has built around himself to protect himself against being recognized and thus expelled. He may hide behind many symptoms of psychological or even physical nature. The condition may not have anything to do with the demon's character directly, but is a result of his presence. The stronghold may be a combination of many feelings, fears, and reactions. It is actually the fortress within which the demon resides and is the means of his protection. With curses broken and strongholds pulled down, the demon has no protection.

While the curse may be broken, the demon cast out, the stronghold must be pulled down by the weapons of our warfare. Do you remember these weapons? They include the blood, the Word, the name of Jesus, our testimony, and our abandonment to the death. These are stronghold destroyers!

These are the three forms of inward oppression, and each of them can be effectively dealt with by the Savior. "Let the oppressed to free!" should be the cry of the church. No gate hell constructs can stand against the church which believes in the power to liberate the captives. Praise the Lord!

9. The Reality of Angels

We now take a serious turn in our study of the victory we have over the devil. We turn away from the devil and his demons to the delightful observation of our allies, the angels. This has been a most neglected area of study in our day. Until recently it was an area of almost total obscurity to me. I must testify that no study has been more delightful than this which has brought to light the glorious provisions of God for the securing and sustaining of our victory over the powers of darkness.

One of the most thrilling sources of study aside from the Bible has been from a discourse by Increase Mather written and published in 1696 entitled *Angelographia*. This discourse was taken from microfilm at some expense and "translated" under great labor (from old English!) He says in the beginning of his treatise, "Angels both good and bad have a greater influence on this world than men are generally aware of. We ought to admire the grace of God toward us sinful creatures in that He hath appointed His Holy Angels to guard us against the mischiefs of wicked spirits who are always intending our hurt both to our bodies and to our souls."

Mrs. George Needham, in her splendid volume, *Angels and Demons,* aptly puts it, "Only slight prominence is accorded to this marvelous truth [angels] in modern Christian teaching. Hence, as is the case with regard to other doctrines, *those who are dimly apprehended by the mind are feebly appreciated by the heart.* Neglecting to study the ministry of angels, the church of God has become impoverished in her experiences of divine providences, and destitute of the succor and comfort which it is her appointed office to supply."

The chapters comprising this division cannot be an exhaustive treatment of angelology. This is not the time or place. There have been and will be volumes given to this task. This is an observation of angels in their capacity of ministering to the children of God in the area of gaining and maintaining victory over the powers of darkness. We will learn together what we need to know about them in order to facilitate and preserve the glorious victory that is rightfully ours.

Could our eyes be opened to the spirit world we would see more than evil spirits and strongholds of wickedness. We would see our allies above us, around us, behind us, and before us. We would see them defending us from the onslaughts of the enemy, protecting our homes, businesses, and travel. We would see them encamped around those that fear the Lord. We would be encouraged, challenged, comforted, and joyously surprised. THE ANGELS ARE WITH US! We may deny them or simply disregard them . . . but they are with us! We may recognize them or completely overlook them . . . but they are with us! By the multiplied thousands and millions they are with us. In thousands of specialized capacities, they are with us. In every kind of situation, they are with us. Include them in your thinking, thank God for them, enjoy them, and employ them.

Let us ask and answer several questions regarding the angels:

Who are they?—They are ministering spirits (Heb. 1:14). God created them in all probability before he created the world. Job 37:4-7 records the answer of God out of the whirlwind to Job in the form of other questions. He was obviously talking about the creation of the worlds when He asked,

"Who stretched the measuring line?"

"On what were the foundations made to rest?"

"Who laid the cornerstone?"

"When the morning stars sang together and the sons of God shouted for joy" (Job 38:4-7). This was an obvious reference to the angels. They are called here the sons of God. Gabeliein, in his volume entitled *The Angels of God* says that this reference to the angels is made six times in the Old Testament. These references are Genesis 6:2, Job 1:6, Job 37:7, Psalm 29:1, and Psalm 89:6. He further states, "But it must be noted that while the angels are called the Sons of God, they are never called the

Sons of Jehovah or sons of the Lord. In the Hebrew it is always "Son of Elohim" (Elohim is God's Name as Creator) and never "the sons of Jehovah." The Sons of Jehovah are sinners redeemed and brought into the final relationship by redemption. The Sons of Elohim are unfallen beings, Sons of God by creation. The angels are the Sons of God in the first creation; sinners saved by grace are the Sons of God in the new creation."

What was the purpose for the angels being created? The angels serve a multitude of purposes as we will later see. They were created by and for the sovereignty of God for His purposes and ends. They stand to give Him glory and to do His bidding. The psalmist helps us in this answer: "Bless the Lord, ye His angels. . . .

That excel in strength. . . .

That do His commandments. . . .

Hearkening unto the voice of His Word" (Psalm 103:20).

How can we know that they are still active in this era of grace? If we had nothing but Scripture in the Old Testament and Scripture in Revelation, we could know beyond a doubt that angels have been active in every period until now and will be active all through the period described in Revelation. Knowing this, we could be safe in assuming that the angels are active in the present as well. With the rest of the New Testament at our disposal we can, however, do much more than *assume*. We can, in fact, *assert* that angels are with us and for us! The writer of Hebrews says, "Are they not all ministering spirits *sent forth to minister* for them who shall be heirs of salvation?" (Heb. 1:14). We shall later see that in Scripture as well as in recent times we have the unimpeachable record of the ministry of angels now.

Can angels communicate with men?—The answer is obviously, YES. The very name in the Greek language suggests "messenger." In Old Testament as well as New Testament times, they conveyed messages from God to man. This does not seem as necessary today as then, because we have the written Word of God to us. However, let us not count them out as being available to God for any special mission he assigns to them for us. It must be remembered that the disciples were delivered from prison when a special angel opened the doors and ordered them to "stand and speak in the temple to the people all the words of this life" (Acts 5:19).

Later on Peter was in prison, and prayer was made in the church for him. An angel (maybe the same locksmith-prison opening angel of Acts 5) awakened Peter, loosened his chains, told him to cast his garment about him and follow him. This he did until he had walked through the last gate and past the last guard. The angel then departed from him. Still later it was Paul who encountered an angel on board ship during a storm. Listen to what he said, "For there stood by me this night an angel of God, whose I am and whom I serve, saying, Fear not, Paul; thou must be brought before Caeser; and, lo, God hath given thee all them that sail with thee" (Acts 27:24).

There are many other questions that we could ask about the angels which would be helpful to satisfy curiosity, but we are not studying to *please the curiosity* but to *preserve the conquest*. And the angels figure very vitally into this conquest. With this in mind let us simply go through the Scripture to seed our minds with the crystals of divine revelation to encourage the showers of comfort-blessings.

The Scriptures from Genesis to Revelation give prominence to angels. They are mentioned by name one hundred and eight times in the Old Testament and one hundred and sixty-five times in the New Testament. There are many other cases where the name "angel" is not mentioned, but we can safely assume that they were on hand. In the following pages we will simply allow the Bible to give us an overall observation of the angels, our allies, at work.

Flaming cherubim (angels) were stationed at the gate of the Garden of Eden to keep the way of the tree of life (Gen. 3:24).

Genesis 16:7-12 records the story of Hagar's rescue at the hands of an angel. (Some believe that this was none other than the preincarnate Son of God, and it may well have been.)

Angels announced the destruction of Sodom. "And when the morning arose, then the angels hastened Lot, saying, Arise, take thy wife and thy two daughters, which are here; lest those be consumed in the iniquity of the city" (Gen. 18:16). The angels then rescued Lot and administered destruction to the cities.

When Abraham was about to sacrifice his son, Isaac, an angel of the Lord "called to him out of heaven" (Gen. 22:11). The angel spoke to him on behalf of God, conveying a message of God's pleasure. The angel spoke a second time in verse 15, with a promised blessing from Jehovah.

As we move through these experiences of ancient times and people, it is wise to put yourself in their places and understand that the same angels which helped them are our helpers today. Praise the Lord! Perhaps one reason for the record of their accomplishments in behalf of the children of God is for our reassurance.

Angels even look after us when we are rebellious. They followed Jacob and were visualized in a dream as recorded in Genesis 28:12, "And he dreamed, and behold a ladder set upon the earth, and the top of it reached to heaven: and behold the angels of God ascending and descending upon it." Here is a picture of the angels going between heaven and earth in service of God in behalf of man. Here is a picture of the abundant life provided for all of God's children. God allowed Jacob to see the kind of life that could be his if his life was yielded to Him. Jacob made a superficial commitment that pivoted around the fickle "if" and went on his backsliding ways.

The angels, however, did not leave Jacob. Another angel spoke to him in Genesis 31:11, telling him to return to the land of his kindred. In Genesis 32 the angels of God met him as he went on his way. This man had a purpose to fulfil in the plan of God, and the angels refused to concede defeat to the devil. They are tenacious indeed! Praise the Lord! Jacob, in his blessing of Joseph in Genesis 48 said, "God, before whom my fathers Abraham and Isaac did walk, the God which fed me all my life long unto this day, THE ANGEL WHICH REDEEMED ME FROM

EVIL, bless the lads" (vv. 15-16). Jacob recognized the work of the angel.

An angel of the Lord appeared to Moses in a flame of fire in the burning bush (Ex. 3:2). God later spoke to him, but he first got his attention through the means of a burning bush and a visualized angel.

We are apt to miss so many cases of angelic help and leadership if we are not looking for it in the Scriptures. It is amazing what a vital role angels played in the life of the people of God in the Old Testament. Angels surely encamped around the whole population of the children of Israel as they began their trek out and continued it. "And the angel of God, which went before the camp of Israel, removed and went behind them, and the pillar of cloud went from before their face, and stood behind them; and it came between the camp of the Egyptians and the camp of Israel; and it was a cloud and darkness to them, but it gave light by night to these; so that the one came not near the other all the night" (Ex. 14:19-20).

God promised the children of Israel that He would send His angel before them to keep their way and to bring them to the place which He had prepared for them (Gen. 23:20). God gave implicit instructions to "beware of him, obey his voice, and provoke him not." Reference is made again to this angel in Exodus 32:34.

Abraham told Isaac, "God will send His angel before thee, and thou shalt take a wife unto my son from thence." It gives me joy to know that as God provided angels for Isaac, He provides them for my Timmy and Tammy. And how we need the angels' help in a world like ours!

Many times an angel is sent by the Lord to keep us from doing something which will get us into serious trouble. This was the case with Balaam in Numbers 22. This is a most interesting study revealing the preventing power of an angel. Balaam was making a forbidden journey. The Word says, "And God's anger was kindled because he went; and the angel of the Lord stood as an adversary against him. Now he was riding upon his ass, and his

82

two servants were with him" (Num. 22:22). In the drama that followed, the ass saw what the rebellious prophet could not see, namely an angel of the Lord standing in the way with a sword drawn. Three times the animal turned from the angel, and three times Balaam beat the animal. Then there was a conversation between the donkey and Balaam! Listen to that conversation:

DONKEY: "What have I done that you have smitten me three times?"

BALAAM: "Because you have mocked me. If I had a sword right now, I would kill you!"

DONKEY: "Am I not yours and have you not ridden ever since I became yours. Do I have a habit of doing such as this to you?"

BALAAM: "No."

Then the eyes of Balaam were opened and he saw the angel. The angel informed him that if the ass had not turned from her way he would have slain Balaam and saved her alive. Balaam repented and obeyed the angel's instructions to go on with the men, but to "speak only the word that I shall speak unto thee" (Num. 22:35).

An angel instructed God's people against idolary in Judges 2:1-5. The angel indicated that he had been with them as they left Egypt and remained with them to bring them into the land that belonged to them. Had their eyes been opened to see, perhaps the Israelites would have seen their great host outnumbered by a host of heaven caring for their needs as they obeyed the Lord. Well might we see the same thing!

An angel of the Lord came to Gideon and said to him, "The Lord is with thee, thou mighty man of valour!" The angel had seen something in him that he had not seen in himself! Our angels must see the same. They see what we can be. The angel continued his conversation with Gideon until Gideon prepared dinner for his guest. They didn't need a fire because the angel's staff caused fire to come out of the rock and consumed what Gideon had prepared. It was after the angel departed that Gideon realized that he had conversed with an angel of God (Jud. 6:11-22).

A most interesting appearance of an angelic messenger appears in the case of Mr. and Mrs. Manoah in Judges 13. An angel announced to Mrs. Manoah that she would bear a son and instructions were given as to how he would be raised. She referred to the angel as "a man of God, whose countenance was like the countenance of an angel, very terrible." When she informed Manoah, he requested that the man of God come again and teach them what they should do.

Again the angel appeared and talked with Mrs. Manoah, but Manoah was not with her. This time when she told Manoah he came, and the angel was still there. The angelic instructions were repeated. Manoah then entreated the angel to stay for lunch. The angel refused, but required an offering to the Lord. Manoah tried to find out the angel's name, but the angel refused to give it. Manoah then prepared the offering, the angel set it afire miraculously, and ascended in the flame of the altar.

In the ensuing events Samson was born. There unfolds a study of sordid affairs, rebellious escapades, tantrums of vindictiveness, and deepening distress on the part of the lad that was destined to be God's man. It is not likely that the angels left their attendance at the side of Samson, as rebellious as he was. They surely ministered to him in the prison and nurtured him back to health and strength for the final victory over the enemy in which he lost his life.

The pestilence which killed seventy thousand men recorded in 2 Samuel 24:15 was administered by an angel of the Lord. When the angel came to Jerusalem and raised his hand to destroy it also, the Lord stopped him and said, "It is enough; stay now thine hand" (2 Sam. 24:16). Thus we see that angels are used in the administration of justice and punishments, but must work under the approval and commandment of the Lord. When David saw this angel, he cried to the Lord in repentance.

Elijah, tired from his long run from Jezreel to Beersheba (almost a hundred miles), sat down under a juniper tree and requested death for himself. He then went to sleep, and an angel subsequently awakened him. The angel had prepared him a meal which he ate. After another nap the angel awakened him again and instructed him after another meal as to the greatness of the journey which faced him. This gourmet angel must have prepared foods that we have no access to, for the strength he gained from that meal lasted for forty days (1 Kings 19:8). We are seeing that the angels have all types of abilities.

Elisha was a hunted man, because of the use that God had made of him against the army of the Syrians. The king of Syria sent an entire army to Dothan to capture him. When the servant of Elisha awoke, he saw the Syrian army surrounding the town and reported the plight to his master. Elisha simply said, "Fear not, *for they that be with us* are more than they that be with them."

Now, I am sure that the poor servant was puzzled. The they-that-be-with-them army was quite visible! Where was the they-that-be-with-us army? That is the reason for the writing of this chapter. Many readers will come to this chapter having seen only the *they-that-be-with-them problem.* May God help your eyes to be opened to the *they-that-be-with-us provisions!* Well, God answered the prayer of Elisha, and the servant saw the mountains full of horses and chariots of fire. The angels had done it again!

When Daniel was thrown into the lion's den he was kept safe until the next morning. He reported to the king that God sent an angel to shut the lions' mouths. How versatile are the angels! Daniel was thus taken from the lions' den unhurt. The angel came out of the lions' den with him, and the lions retained their former disposition. This is clearly revealed. We see the men who had accused Daniel thrown into the den with their wives and children. The Scripture said, "The lions had the mastery of them, and brake all their bones in pieces before they came to the bottom of the den" (Dan. 6:24).

This was not the last experience that Daniel was to have with an angel. Gabriel appeared to him in Chapter 9 and said, "O Daniel, I am now come forth to give thee skill and understanding."

Then Gabriel proceeded to tell Daniel what would shortly come to pass. He informed Daniel that he was a man greatly beloved.

Following this experience Daniel went on a fast which was to last for twenty-one days. On the last day an angel came to him and informed him that his prayer had been heard from the first day, but that he was supernaturally detained by a battle with the prince of the kingdom of Persia. He reported that Michael, the archangel, had helped him win the victory over the devil's strong angel along with Daniel's prayers (Dan. 10:12). The angel spoke and Daniel was strengthened. That same angel declared that he had stood with Darius to confirm and strengthen him. We behold, then, that God's angels help even the heathen leaders in the interest of God's plan through the ages. We can be sure then that behind every era of history God's angels are guarding the scene. Despite everything that the devil and his demons can do to the contrary, God's will is done.

The angels are the "watchers" and the "holy ones" mentioned in Daniel 4:17. "The matter is by the decree of the *watchers* and the demand of the *holy ones;* to the intent that the living may know that the Most High ruleth in the kingdom of men, and giveth it to whomsoever he will, and settest it over the basest of men."

The living creatures of Ezekiel's vision were doubtlessly angels. They were mighty, dreadful creatures with eyes all around. Their wings made a great noise and their voices were as the voice of a great host (Ezek. 1:24). These fearful, dreadful angels are alive today with undaunted power and are ever at God's disposal!

Just as angels can protect, they can destroy. One angel entered the Assyrian army which was encamped against Jerusalem and left 185,000 soldiers dead (2 Kings 19:35). That angel, my friend, is still with us and is one of our allies! Praise the Lord! Did you hear that, Satan?

Zechariah carried on conversations with angels and they helped him write his prophetic message (Zech. 1:9,12,14,19). In fact an angel is mentioned no less than twenty times in the first six chapters of the book of Zechariah.

These references make up only a part of the great list of angel listings. Just as we have seen that the devil is highly organized and has demons who are specialists in all areas of life and all levels of responsibility, we may be sure God has the same and *much more!* Already we have encountered all sorts of angels . . .

> lock-picking angels (disciples in prison)
> chain-loosing angels (Peter in prison)
> birth announcement angels (Samson's parents)
> rescue angels (Hagar in wilderness)
> warning angels (to Lot)
> destroying angels (Sodom)
> guarding angels (Garden of Eden)
> leading angels (Israelites)
> death angels (Assyrian army)
> lion-taming angels (Daniel)
> prophetic angels (Zechariah)
> warring angels (Elisha)
> gourmet angels (Elijah)

and rebuking angels (Balaam). And these are only a few of the mentions of the hosts of heaven!

Joshua met the *captain* of the hosts of the Lord as recorded in Joshua 5:13-15. This is doubtless a reference to the preincarnate Son of God. Jesus is the captain of the angelic hosts. They listen to His command and do His bidding. When Joshua got in line with the captain, the hosts under the captain were at his disposal! And so with us! Praise the Lord!

We observe further that the reserves of the Father are limitless. The number of angels is not given, but several hints as to the vastness of their number are given:

Job asks, "Is there any number of his armies?" (Job 25:2).

Daniel reported, "Thousand thousands ministered unto him, and ten thousand times ten thousand stood before him" (Dan. 7:10). This assures us that there are more than 100 million angels.

The psalmist said, "Great was the company that published it; the chariots of God are twenty thousand, even thousands of angels" (Ps. 68:11,17).

In Hebrews we further read, "But ye are come unto Mount Zion, and unto the city of the living God, the heavenly Jerusalem, and to *an innumerable company of angels.*"

In Revelation we see multiplied thousands of angels. John saw millions of angels as well and "thousands of thousands" (Rev. 5: 11).

Jesus suggested to Peter that he could call on the Father who would "presently" give him more than twelve legions of angels. By conservative estimates that would be around 70,000 angels. They were waiting and available to come under Christ's command. Those same angels are available to us. They are under his authority (1 Pet. 3:22). Though we were made a little lower than the angels, they have been sent to be our helpers. There are plenty of them and to spare!

The psalmist affirms in 34:7 that, "The angel of the Lord encampeth around about them that fear him, and delivereth him." He featured that an angel would chase and persecute his enemies (35:5-6). He revealed that "man did eat angels' food" (78:25, an obvious reference to the manna in the wilderness). The protection of the angels is promised in Psalm 34:10-12, "There shall no evil befall thee, neither shall any plague come near thy dwelling. FOR HE SHALL GIVE HIS ANGELS CHARGE OVER THEE, TO KEEP THEE IN ALL THY WAYS. They shall bear thee up in their hands, lest thou dash thy foot against a stone." Is this not good news, dear friend, for the living of these days?

That the existence and employment of the angels has much to do with spiritual warfare and thus spiritual victory is a fact assumed in the Scriptures. Miss Corrie ten Boom says that when we talk about the devil or demons for five miuntes, we should talk about the angels for twice as long. How much more attention we need to pay our allies in the spirit warfare. They are our allies to strengthen us and to continuously support us. It is unthinkable that God should provide the hosts of heaven to care for the saints of other ages and abandon us to the battle alone with the devil and his angels!

It is not likely, however, that people in general, will become mindful of the ministry of angels until they become mindful of the state of war that exists between the power of darkness and our Lord. Mrs. Needham in *Angels and Demons* says, " 'Where is the necessity of angelic ministry?' " some ask in this self-confident and comfortable church of God. The perils of Egypt and the pilgrimage of Israel pertain not to us. No autocratic monarch menaces our Christian liberty by fiery furnace or savage beast. No Syrian hosts encompass us around. We are at 'ease in Zion,' and 'Jerusalem is a quiet habitation.' Thus has the church been a long time vaunting itself, while the angels of God, unrecognized and undesired, appear to have refrained their precious offices, and withheld their visitations, even as of old they once left Jacob to his carnal plans and fleshly fears."

It is my growing conviction that we need to be much better acquainted with our allies, the angels.

Some may pass their existence into antiquity by saying, "Yes, but that was in the Old Testament." We have already set forth some cases in apostolic times of the action of angels in opening prison doors and conveying messages. Some may even say in response to this that this was in the days of transitional truths and such is not in order for us today. To this we may say that angels have continued their ministry through every transition! There was not one period when they did not minister at the bidding of God. We have no solid reason to conclude that their existence or ministry ceased with the advent of modern intellect. Indeed we have greatly limited their ministry by refusing to give them heed, but their existence is still a reality and they wait to aid us.

There may be some concern that we may boost the reputation of the angels above that of the Holy Spirit. It has pleased God in His economy to use the manifestations of the Godhead and the angels in such a way as never to be in conflict. Elijah was *filled* with the Spirit, but fed by the angel. Peter was *liberated* by the Spirit from the law, but *let out* of prison by an angel. Paul was a man controlled by the Spirit, and yet an angel gave him a special message about the safety of the crew of the ill-fated ship. The ministry of the Holy Spirit in no way precludes the value of the help of the angels.

This is the age of the ministry of the Spirit, and it is probable that angelic availability has not lessened during these days of grace. If the ministry of angels seems less evident and effectual during these days, it is doubtlesly our fault. Just suppose that an employer needed the help of a dozen men, asked for that help, and received it. The *availability* of those men as they reported to work would not guarantee their maximum value. If the employer refused to acknowledge the fact that they were on the job, their effectiveness would be greatly hindered if not completely destroyed. Likewise, as much value as the angels have to us, their effectiveness in our behalf will never be greater than our awareness of them. Because of the failure of our sophisticated society to acknowledge these blessed spirit beings and their availability to us, millions of them are eager, but hindered in doing the service for us that they so love to do. They are *all* ministering spirits, sent forth to minister for them who shall be the heirs of salvation (Heb. 1:14).

Can you feature in the spirit realm hundreds of thousands of spirits with abilities with which ours cannot compare waiting to serve you? Can you imagine having at your aid one as strong as an army, as wise as a thousand sages, as concerned as a long-beloved friend, as swift and as splendid as the wind? Would you be interested in such a helper as this? Well, we have such helpers by the host, and yet we are busy denying their existence by the way we live!

Now I want to increase your awareness of the angels and their work until you are asking, "How can I make the most of their availability?" The answer to that question will come in the next chapter. But before we come to that chapter, I want to discuss with you the work of these messengers in two realms. First in the realm just preceding this dispensation, specifically in the ministry of Jesus and second, in the last things of Revelation. This will serve to sandwich us into the relatively narrow segment of time with angel influence on either side and should make us aware of the glorious fact that THIS IS THE DAY TO BE ALIVE!

Angels in the Life of Jesus

An angel announced the birth of John the Baptist and gave the name that he was to have (Luke 1:13).

Gabriel was sent by God to Nazareth to speak to Mary. He spoke to her in clear terms about the plans of God for her. When she was afraid, he reassured her and explained further. He answered her questions and explained in further detail the birth of John the Baptist. When she had committed herself saying, "Be it unto me according to thy word," the angel departed. Matthew records the angel's visit to Joseph much later, after Mary was found to be with child. The angel said, "Fear not to take unto thee Mary thy wife: for that which is conceived in her is of the Holy Ghost. And she shall bring forth a son, and thou shalt call his name JESUS: for he shall save his people from their sins" (Matt. 1:20-21).

Angels were used to announce the birth of Jesus to the shepherds. First the angel came upon them and the light was bright around them as he made the announcement, "FOR UNTO YOU IS BORN THIS DAY IN THE CITY OF DAVID A SAVIOUR, WHICH IS CHRIST THE LORD!" Then a host of angels got in on the celebration as they joined in a chorus of praise saying, "GLORY TO GOD IN THE HIGHEST, AND ON EARTH PEACE, GOOD WILL TOWARD MEN" (Luke 2:11,13).

An angel warned Joseph to flee to Egypt, knowing of the action that Herod would take to try to take the child's life. He stated that he would give him further word at the proper time (Matt. 2:13). When Herod was dead, the angel reappeared to Joseph and ordered him to return to the land of Israel.

We know very little of the life of Jesus from childhood to thirty years. It does not take imagination to assume that his whole life was surrounded by angelic protection and help. How Satan would have loved to destroy Him! But God had hedged Him about by the hosts of heaven, and Satan could not touch Him without divine permission.

When Jesus was led of the Spirit into the wilderness to be tempted by the devil, the angel stood by. After the struggle was over and Jesus had won, the angels came and ministered to Him. Can you imagine how meticulous and eager the angels were who waited on the Son of God? They must have crowded around him with greater excitement than the crowd around a recently crowned champion. They ministered to him! That simply means that where there was a need, there was a minister. They were there to serve him, and what service angels can render!

A special angel came to Jesus in the Garden of Gethsemane. The Bible simply says, "And there appeared an angel unto him from heaven, strengthening him" (Luke 22:42). How I would love to know what that angel did! The angel who ministered to Daniel just spoke a word, and Daniel received strength. It was immediately after the angel strengthened him that he prayed the more earnestly until his sweat became as blood. THE ANGEL HAD STRENGTHENED HIM FOR PRAYER. Angels are our prayer helpers!

We read no more of angel help between Gethsemane and Calvary. They must fold their wings and back away. Jesus must tread the lonesome path alone. Not even an angel can move along this path! And so He goes alone. But at the appointed time an angel comes from heaven and with his coming there is an earthquake. And that angel whose coming caused the earth to shake, rolled back the stone from the door and sat on it! Matthew described him thus, "His countenance was like lightning, and his raiment white as snow; and for fear of him the keepers did shake, and became as dead men. And the angel answered and said unto the women, FEAR NOT YE; for I know that ye seek Jesus, which is crucified. He is not here; for he is risen, as he said. Come see the place where he lay. And go quickly and tell his disciples that he is risen from the dead; and behold, he goeth forth before you into Galilee; there shall ye see him: lo, I have told you" (Matt. 28:3-7).

John's Gospel records the experience of Mary Magdalene coming to the tomb and seeing two angels in white sitting where the body of Jesus had been. They asked, "Woman, why weepest thou?" When she had answered and turned around, she saw Jesus Himself (John 20:12-13).

It may have been those same two angels who were present at the ascension of Jesus. It seems that in both cases both of them speak the same thing. As Jesus is taken up in a cloud, which could well be a host of angels, the angels said, "Ye man of Galilee, why stand ye gazing up into heaven? This same Jesus which is taken up from you into heaven, shall so come in like manner as ye have seen him go into heaven." Thus, angels became the *blessed hope* of the church.

Jesus Taught About Angels

Not only did angels surround the path of Jesus and minister to Him, but angels formed a vital point of discussion in His ministry.

Jesus promised that if we confessed Him before men, He would confess us before the Father in the presence of the angels (Luke 12:8).

He referred to little ones and "their angels" which implies that every child has a guardian angel (Matt. 18:10).

He pictured the angels as rejoicing over one sinner that repents (Luke 15:10).

As He told the story of the beggar and the rich man, He said the angels carried the beggar to Abraham's bosom. They remain our helpers through the experience of death (Luke 16:22).

In the end Jesus will send forth His angels to gather out of the kingdom all things that offend and them which do iniquity AND SHALL CAST THEM INTO A FURNACE OF FIRE: there shall be wailing and gnashing of teeth (Matt. 13:41-42).

Jesus told Peter that he could have notified the Father and twelve legions of angels would have come to rescue Him. Jesus knew that they were available. How often He must be disappointed at our puny efforts when such power is standing by (Matt. 26:53).

ALL the angels will come with Jesus when He comes (Matt.

16:27; 25:31). He went with a cloud and He will come with a cloud—millions of angels! What a day that will be!

Paul tells us that when Jesus comes in the rapture the archangel's voice will be heard (1 Thess. 4:16). I wonder what he will say. It will be the shout heard round the world.

Angels in Revelation

The Book of Revelation is full of angels, here an angel, there an angel, everywhere an angel! There are millions of angels and single angels, angels with good news and angels with bad news. They are given mention approximately sixty times in Revelation. It will suffice to merely list some of the significant roles of the angels in the book:

An angel was the intermediary between God and John for the writing of the book (Rev. 1:1).

A strong angel sought One who would open the book with seven seals (Rev. 5:2).

One hundred million angels (plus) shouted, "WORTHY IS THE LAMB THAT WAS SLAIN TO RECEIVE POWER AND RICHES, AND HONOUR, AND GLORY, AND BLESSING" (Rev. 5:11-12). What a choir!

An angel administered the prayers of the saints (Rev. 8:3-5).

Seven angels loosed seven trumpets (Rev. 8:6,7).

Four angels loosed the two hundred million horsemen (Rev. 9:15,16).

Flying angels proclaimed the gospel and the fall of Babylon (Rev. 14:6,8).

Seven angels loosed the seven plagues (Rev. 15:1).

An angel presided over the destruction of the beast (Rev. 19:17).

An angel bound Satan (Rev. 20:12)!

An angel showed John the New Jerusalem (Rev. 21:9).

Twelve angels guarded the gates to the New Jerusalem (Rev. 21:19).

An angel forbade John to worship him (Rev. 22:9).

Thus, it is obvious that we are surrounded in history by angels!

They have ever been attentive to the needs of the earth. They do not die, so we may conclude that every angel that has ever been available for divine service and human help is still available.

Compared to the demons of the devil, they are mightier in number. Many of the wicked spirits that fell from heaven are in chains and thus are not free to roam the earth. We know that only one third of heaven's hosts chose to rebel with Satan. Thus, heaven's hosts greatly outnumber the hosts of hell. Not only do they outnumber the demons, but they are more powerful because they represent the greater power of God. They move under His authority, and the devil cannot contest it.

We are enjoined to "be not forgetful to entertain strangers; for thereby some have entertained angels unawares" (Heb. 1:1).

The angels are with us and figure vitally into victory over the devil!

10. The Recognition of Angels

So there are angels! What do we do? How can we take advantage of their existence for the glory of God and the good of man? How do they help us in the victory over the devil? What is our relationship to them? How shall we react to them?

As we come to know the nature and purpose of the angels, it is not difficult to know what to do to derive the most benefit from their existence. But as we come to ackowledge the presence of angels in our age, we must be careful lest we swing the pendulum to a dangerous extreme on the other side. It would be easy to come from complete denial to angel worship. This is expressly forbidden in the scripture. "Let no man beguile you of your reward in a voluntary humility and WORSHIPPING OF ANGELS" (Col. 2:18).

When John fell at the feet of the angel in Revelation 19, the angel said, "See thou do it not; I am thy fellow-servant, and of thy brethren that have the testimony of Jesus: WORSHIP GOD; For the testimony of Jesus is the spirit of prophecy" (Rev. 19: 10). So we are not to worship angels or pray to them.

Then what are we to do?

We are to acknowledge them.—This is a good beginning. They are helpers to all who would be the heirs of salvation. It is significant to note here that they are helpers for the heirs of salvation. They have not been sent just to minister to, but *to* minister *for* (Heb. 1:14). Just the mere recognition that they exist encourages the angels in their particular ministries in our behalf. Nothing is more limiting for them than total disregard. As we acknowledge their presence in all types of situations, God is able to utilize them to a greater degree in our safety and benefit. We are to acknowledge them in keeping our possessions, in guarding us in travel, and in watching our homes. We can safely assume that they care for the church and are looking after its welfare.

We are to praise the Lord for them.—Is it not heartening to realize that God has assigned us to the care of the angels who can bear us up in their hands, camp round about us, and place themselves at our disposal. Then we can thank Him for our guardian angels and for special angels assigned to us in special times of need. As we praise the Lord, his power is released so much the more, and their work is that much easier.

We are to pray.—I have a feeling that angels are ever listening to us. Though we do not pray to the angels, when we pray the angels are alerted and ready to go to work because of our prayers. They love to work at that to which they are called, namely the welfare of the people of God. When we pray we can ask God to dispatch angels to do special things. I want to share with you a few stories which bear the value of praying in this manner.

I was praying one night with some dear friends when God placed a friend on my heart who lived in another area more than two hundred and fifty miles away. As I prayed I asked the Lord how He wanted me to pray for her. She had been the victim of a satanic attack in her family, and things had been quite distressing in her life. I was led to pray just a simple prayer like this, "Lord make known your presence and send your angelic messengers to surround her home and to fill it with your glory." We all prayed briefly for her and left it at that.

In less than twenty-four hours she was sitting in front of my desk in my study. She said, "Brother Jack, the strangest thing happend to me last night. My little boy was crying over our situation. He finally slipped off to sleep, but continued to sob in his fitful sleep. My heart was broken for him, and I began to pray, knowing that God could heal the situation. I had no sooner gotten the word, "Lord" out of my mouth than he settled down in a deep sleep. It seemed to me then that the room was filled with angels and that there were angels all around the house."

"I asked her when this experience took place. She related the time and it was exactly the same time that we were praying for her! A strange coincidence? I think not!

A precious little girl in our church had developed a fear, because of some strange antics going on in the neighborhood. The door bell would ring, and there would be no one there. The screen on her window had been found cut. It had been months since she had been able to sleep through the night. The situation became quite distressing to her parents.

One night she awakened with great fear. We had been talking about the devil and angels in our study at church. The mother decided to put some of what she had learned to work. She resisted the devil and refused the fear that the devil was giving the daughter. They then prayed together that God would dispatch His angels to look after the house and keep her safe.

While they were still praying the little daughter said, "Mother, do you hear them, do you hear them?" The mother heard nothing but the little girl continued to hear them. The mother asked what she was hearing. She replied that she was hearing the angels sing. When asked what they were singing, she said, "They are singing, Peace, Peace!" She said they sang to her all night and she slept the night through. Her fears were gone and she

97

slept soundly thereafter.

Another of our ladies was in the hospital and underwent major surgery. She remarked to her husband what wonderful care she was getting and that all night long nurses were lined up around her bed tending to her every need. When the husband investigated it was found that she was getting along so very well that very few nurse visits were needed. Yet she insisted that all through the hours following surgery they were there. I believe that they were—the angels, that is!

While I am telling stories, I cannot leave this one out. One of our staff members, Mrs. Cade, our church visitor and a great soul winner, had an automobile accident and her car was in the shop for weeks. It was a necessity that she have an automobile to continue her visitation and yet there was one part that could not be found anywhere for her car. She brought up this problem in staff meeting. I exclaimed, almost facetiously, that God knew exactly where the part could be found and that if we asked Him to, He would just dispatch one of His auto-parts angels to find it. We found ourselves praying that the Lord would send an angel to find the part and get it to San Antonio quickly. Would you believe that within two hours the part was found and on its way to San Antonio and they had been searching for it for several weeks!

Praying encourages and aids the angels. It was through the help of Daniel's prayer and the strength of Michael that the angel got through. We have no idea what effect our praying has on the realms where the spiritual battles are being fought, but if we knew, we would surely pray more!

We can worship.—Angels can greatly aid our worship. Isaiah stepped in on a worship scene in Isaiah 6 and found himself a part of a glorious worship service. The seraphim were there worshipping in humility and crying, "Holy, Holy, Holy is the Lord God of Hosts" (Isa. 6:3). Surely the angels are near in the experiences of worship.

We can witness.—Jesus informs us that there is joy among the angels over one sinner that repents. Therefore when we witness, we are engaged in something that is of vital interest to the angels. One of their favorite tasks is certainly that of providing protection to those who are going about witnessing.

We can trust.—How it must grieve the angels when we do not trust the Lord, as they know He can be trusted. They mourn for us and wish for us such a trust that we could abandon ourselves to the Lord. I can feature that when someone decides to really trust the Lord with their lives, the angels take delight to volunteer to accompany that person on the adventure to which he has committed himself.

We can be lawful and careful.—I think some of our guardian angels must be overworked the way some of us drive. Some folks take needless risks and some even break the law. The protection that the angels have to offer may well be withdrawn the moment we pass the speed limit for we have been told as Christians to respect the laws that man has given to govern us. The care of the angels does not place us beyond the need of care and lawfulness.

These are just some suggestions that might enhance your relationship with the messengers from heaven sent to enhance your sojourn on the earth. God is delighted to give you the best of care. He has assigned your external welfare to able spirits, and He abides in you. We are cared for!

If the devil has demons in charge of cities, institutions, businesses, churches, and individuals, then so does God have angels in those same capacities. The angels are here to administer victory. Christ has won the victory, angels help us to sustain the victory, and the devil's attacks are to no avail.

God has angels trained in every area of need that His children will ever experience. He has mechanic-oriented angels for believers with machines that are always breaking down. He has nursing angels for those that are sick. He has angels to protect churches and institutions. While the Holy Spirit cares for the inner needs, God uses the angels to minister in areas of the physical.

Whether we go by means of death into the presence of God or

through the rapture, we will do business with angels. If we die we will be escorted by angels to heaven. Increase Mather in his *Angelographia* tells of several who experienced the coming of the angels at their dying. He says of one faithful minister in New England, "It was a great act of faith in an eminently faithful minister of Christ, about thirty years ago, that when he perceived the approaches of death, he was no way concerned at it; but after he had spoken a few words to those about him, said, 'And now you Holy angels come and do your office.' He had no sooner uttered these words, but he died. Angels were about him and they heard what he said and were ready to conduct his soul into the presence of the Lord Jesus Christ."

He told of another learned and godly man, Dr. Holland, whose last words were, "O thou whose fiery chariots came down to fetch Elijah, you angels that attended the soul of Lazarus, bear me into the bosom of my best beloved!"

And there was another whose dying words were these, "Oh! That you had your eyes opened to see what I see: I see millions of angels: God hath appointed them to carry my soul up to heaven, where I shall behold the Lord face to face."

If we remain until the coming of Jesus, we shall all be changed and caught up immediately with the Lord and His angels, they being the means by which we are gathered together!

What are we to do because there are angels? In closing this chapter let us allow an angel to tell us. The angel spoke in the days of Zechariah saying, "Thus saith the Lord of hosts; If thou wilt walk in my ways, and if thou keep my charge, then thou shalt also judge my house, and shall also keep my courts, AND I WILL GIVE THEE PLACES TO WALK AMONG THESE THAT STAND BY" (Zech. 3:7). And who are these that stand by? The holy angels!

There are angels standing by this day beckoning us to walk with them in the heavenlies. Let us be careful to walk in this manner with the Lord and with His own, knowing that in a very little while, we shall be walking in the galleries of heaven. These angel friends will tell us wonderful things that were done in our behalf, how we were delivered in such and such a place, how we were accompanied in a lonely place, and how they prevented evil plans from being carried out against us.

We will then experience the reality of Revelation 5 where the elders and the angels harmonized in ascribing praise and honour to Jesus, saying BLESSING, HONOUR, AND GLORY UNTO HIM THAT SITS ON THE THRONE, AND UNTO THE LAMB FOR EVER AND EVER!

In the meanwhile, the angels are our able allies! Praise the Lord for them.

11. Victory Is Now!

"This *IS* the victory that overcomes the world, even our faith" (1 John 5:4).

"But thanks be to God who *IS GIVING* us the victory through our Lord Jesus Christ" (1 Cor. 15:58).

"Nay, in all these things we *ARE* more than conquerors through Him that loved us" (Rom. 8:37).

"Now thanks be to God Who *ALWAYS CAUSES* us to triumph in Christ" (2 Cor. 2:14).

"*I AM* the Way, the Truth, and the Life" (John 14:6).

We are not working from defeat to victory, but from victory to victory. Victory is not a point of departure or even a destination. IT IS A WAY OF GOING. It does not rest on what we are, have done, or are doing. It rests on Him—the Lord Jesus Christ who is the VICTOR. In short, since victory is a way of going and Jesus is the way, VCTORY IS SIMPLY JESUS CHRIST. You cannot have victory without a victor.

"Christ is living the victorious life today; and Christ is your life. Let Him do it all. Your effort or trying had nothing to do with the salvation which you have in Christ; in exactly the same way your effort and trying can have nothing to do with the complete victory which Christ alone has achieved for you and can

101

steadily achieve in you" (Charles Trumbull).

"Victory is ever and only God's order of the day. It is something we already possess. It is the Christian's right as truly as the air he breathes. However, he must understand the conditions. He must see himself enthroned with Christ. He must see himself according to God's own Holy Word, as crucified with Christ, dead, buried, raised and made to sit in heavenly places with his Lord and Saviour, Jesus Christ" (F. J. Huegel).

It is impossible to *get* something you already *have*. This is the reason that many people are not walking in victory. They are seeking an experience in which something which they do not have will become theirs. What do you have need of that you do not have? Think on the answer for a moment. You will find yourself thinking of many things that you do not *apparently* have, that is they have not become obvious to you. You will find, regardless of how long and deeply you think, that you cannot think of anything that you do not already have. *"Christ is all"* (Col. 2:10). "For in him dwelleth all the fulness of the Godhead bodily" (Col. 2:9).

We have the victory because we have Him who has won the victory. Our faith in Him brings the victory which is already in us to light. As we reckon it continuously by faith, He continues to make it real.

But alas, dear reader, this does not mean that you are walking now in victory! In fact, it may be that at this very hour you have been confronted by a problem of such nature that your victory is seemingly gone. You are thinking, "If this is victory, I wonder what defeat is like!" To have victory as a *possession* does not mean that you have victory as a *practice*.

You can own a Cadillac and walk!

You can have groceries and go hungry!

You can have friends and be lonely!

You can have the Holy Spirit and be motivated by the devil!

YOU CAN HAVE THE VICTORY AND BE LIVING IN DE-
FEAT!

It is a matter of . . .

ACKNOWLEDGING YOUR VICTORY TO BE IN JESUS,
APPROPRIATING IT BY FAITH'S ACT,
ASSERTING IT BY FAITH'S WORD,
AND APPLYING IT THROUGH FAITH'S
DEMONSTRATION!

We have the victory, but it is a matter of GOING, KNOWING,
AND GROWING! Just as Joshua had the victory when he stood
at Gilgal, so we have the victory when we stand in faith to assert
that we have it. But just as a mighty land was spread out before
him with enemies who would contest every acre of ground, so we
must ready ourselves for *sustaining* the victory we already have
and *spreading* that victory to wherever the Lord leads.

This life is a RIVER, not a pool. A river is *fresh* and *flowing;*
a pool can become *static* and *stagnant*. When victory becomes
static, it is no longer victory.

The promise of Jesus is, "If any man thirst, let him come unto
me and drink. He that believeth on me as the scriptures hath
said, OUT OF HIS BELLY SHALL FLOW RIVERS OF LIV-
ING WATER" (John 7:37-38). There is nothing static about
that promise!

So victory has the NOWNESS of a mighty flowing river,
a roaring waterfall,
of a marching army,
of a singing multitude,
of a million candlepower lamp,
ever in the present tense, *now,* but ever continuing!

God *is!* His grace *is!* "AS HE IS SO ARE WE IN THIS
WORLD" (1 John 4:17).

But in the midst of victory, we must not forget that there are
obstacles, opposition, and a foe to face, fight, and overcome.
Knowing and doing so will keep victory in the *NOW!*

12. Menaces to the Maintenance of Victory

The enemy is not content to let us float along on the tide of uncontested victory. It was not so with Joshua in Canaan, and it will not be so with us. We will be opposed and contested. The devil will *attempt* it for the *defeat* of our faith. God will allow it for the *demonstration* of our faith. It is well that we know the "lay of the land" as we move through it in victory. Let us observe some areas where victory has vanished for many.

Man's System

Man's system since the fall has been contrary to God's. Man's system would build a tower that reaches to heaven. God's system brings heaven down to man. Man's system is largely built on what man can do for God. God's system is built on what He has done and is doing for us. Man's system is try, try, try. God's system is trust, trust, trust.

There are thousands of people today floundering after a joyous revelation of life of victory, because they are trying to gear the dynamics of the resurrection life to the designs of the human system. This is the reason that when resurrection life invades the average church, there is immediate trouble. I would not advocate revolution on the human plane, but I must warn you. If you seek to apply the terms of victory in Christ to the machinery built around flesh, you will not only fail in the realm of service, but you will lose your own sense of victory. Must we then destroy the system? No! We must allow the life of the Resurrected Lord to flow through the system until every part is touched and taken over by His life. What is needless will be superfluous and will flake away. What is needed will remain.

Man's Vision

If we believe only what we can see with our natural eyes, we will fail. Until we *see* the *invisible,* we will not *do* the *impossible.*

Every man who has come to discouragement and defeat has done so because he did not see the invisible. His vision was limited to the visible. There are two clear illustrations of the negative and the positive of this truth. First, there was *Elijah,* who believed the devil's lie that his life was in danger. He believed the visible and disbelieved the invisible. Having viewed the problem and not the power, he took off running. He ran almost a hundred miles before he stopped, and then he was too tired to think. He was in the pit of discouragement, viewing only the visible.

What he didn't see was that God was a God of limitless power. There were 7,000 people who had never bowed to kiss Baal's toe! He didn't see a young man ploughing, waiting to be enlisted into God's army. He didn't see the coming miracles that God would accomplish through him. He never would have seen if he had not believed and obeyed and followed the Lord. As long as *fear* for the *visible* remains, *faith* in the *invisible* is stifled. If you are discouraged today and living in defeat it is because you are *receiving fear* and *refusing faith.* Turn the procedure around and God's victory will break through.

Second, there is *Jehoshaphat.* The story is told in 2 Chronicles 20. He was notified about the problem of an invading army of such size that victory in the flesh was out of the question. He refused to station his eyes on the problem. This was his first right decision. He chose to get his eyes on the invisible. He proclaimed a fast and declared himself in prayer—the means of opening the view to the invisible. He then exclaimed, "LORD, WE HAVE NO POWER AGAINST THIS GREAT COMPANY THAT IS COMING AGAINST US: NEITHER KNOW WE WHAT TO DO: *BUT OUR EYES* ARE ON YOU!" (2 Chron. 20:12).

Have you ever thought what might have happened if Jehoshaphat had kept his eyes on the problem? As long as we keep our eyes on the problem, our resources are limited to the visible. He would have fought the battle as best he could with what he had and have lost! But when man turns his eyes to the PROBLEM SOLVER, the magnitude of our resources swells to the proportion of His riches in glory.

Will we be such fools as to limit the scope of our work to what we can understand, what we can see, and what we can deem possible within the context of common sense? Will we operate on the visible resources, our bank account, our anticipated receipts, and our visible assets when the TREASURY OF THE UNIVERSE IS FULL AND WAITING TO BE TAPPED?

Soulish Experience

Here is a problem which is keener in times of spiritual blessing than in any other season. It is here that balance can be lost in the walk with Christ and victory departed without the slightest suspicion. I can here only sound a warning without seeking to be exhaustive. It is impossible for man to understand the difference between soul and spirit. Only the Word of God can divide them. This is the reason that we must stay in the Word and be filled with the Word, as we are filled with the Spirit. Let me seek to be of help by contrasting soul and spirit.

Soul emphasizes feeling. Spirit emphasizes faith.

Soul operates on emotional experiences. Spirit operates only on spiritual reality, produced by the Holy Spirit.

Soul is preoccupied with one's self. Spirit is preoccupied with Him.

While there are differences, there are also points of sameness. Both soul and spirit are capable of phenomenal demonstrations of power. Psychic discoveries are being made today, which are sidetracking many a Christian in detainment and finally in defeat. There are even areas of religion where there is such preoccupation with the emotions of the experience, that soulish power is being substituted for Spirit power with tragic results.

Andrew Murray said, "The greatest danger the individual has

to dread is the inordinate activity of the soul with its powers of mind and will." This danger is multiplied in our day with the great revival of the occult, which emphasizes the latent powers within men. The danger is further deepened by the emphasis on experiences that must be measured by certain emotions and manifestations in the religious realm.

There are soulish *conversions* in which a man's emotions are moved by soulish displays and soulish methods. There is soulish *joy* that looks inward to the emotions rather than up to the throne. There is soulish *victory* that is light and flighty, but breaks down when stern spiritual realities appear. The time is coming when more and more Christians will either be mesmerized by the devil or filled with the Spirit.

The answer . . . THE WORD OF GOD! "For the Word of God is quick [alive], and sharper than any two-edged sword, PIERCING EVEN TO THE DIVIDING ASUNDER OF SOUL AND SPIRIT" (Heb. 4:12).

Wrong Doctrine

Wrong doctrine is the source of soulish experience, but let us enlarge on the waste of wrong doctrine. I am accustomed to saying that we should not haggle over terminology. I'd rather see someone who had the right thing and called it the wrong thing, than to see someone who called it the right thing and didn't have anything. I do not mean to imply that it doesn't make any difference what terminology we use. To the contrary it makes very much difference.

For instance, any doctrine which implies that salvation is any less than an operation of the Holy Spirit in which one is indwelt by the Spirit of Christ is a false doctrine. I know that you and I both have friends who maintain that there is an experience subsequent to the salvation experience which is called "the baptism in the Holy Spirit" or "receiving the Holy Spirit," but friends or not, they are mistaken. The baptism (of which there is only one) takes place when we are saved. Paul affirmed in 1 Corinthians 12:13, "For by one Spirit are we all baptized into one body." The verb for "baptized" is an aorist verb in the Greek and this implies not only something which has already taken place, but is completed. The "we" includes both Paul and those to whom he was writing.

There is a growing system today which teaches that when one gets "the baptism in the Holy Ghost," he will speak in unintelligible languages as "the" evidence. Afterward when he speaks in these tongues, it will be "the gift of tongues." This is without support in the Scripture. For support of existing experiences, our friends are left to broken logic and proof-texts.

When we are saved, we are baptized in the Holy Spirit. It is a matter of faith, and faith demands no evidence—it *is* evidence (Heb. 11:1)! We are nowhere implored to be baptized in the Holy Spirit. We are enjoined to "be filled with the Holy Spirit" (Eph. 5:18). There is one baptism; there are many fillings. I am not "antigifts," as is proved by a previous volume *Much More*. But I affirm that the gifts are for equipment, not for evidence. The fruit of the Spirit and the accompanying power of God are evidences of the Spirit's fulness.

Many strong men who are considered scholars espouse this doctrine. While they may continue to believe these things and survive, many of those whom they teach suffer spiritual shipwreck, because of the waste of wrong doctrine.

Again, the only answer is to judge every feeling and every experience and every stated doctrine by the Word of God! When we begin to judge the Word by our experiences, we have already gone past the point of no return as far as spiritual safety is concerned.

Weariness in Well-Doing

Many a spiritual giant has been reduced to ruin by something no more serious than the failure to rest his body. Elijah learned that there was only one thing to do when one is tired—that is REST! Prayer and praise are wonderful, but rest is just as necessary. In the room provided for the prophet, there was a bed for rest. I have seen people get on a spiritual high and begin to assume that simply because they are praising the Lord with joy, they are immuned from the laws of the physical. The next thing you know they are down spiritually.

Though the joy of the Lord is our strength, it is a joy to the Lord for us to rest. He, Himself, often went aside from the press of the crowd to rest in the presence of the Father. How much more must we recognize the weakness of the physical and give rest that we might be the vehicles of His righteousness!

Assumed Maturity

Pride has taken a high toll in Christian circles. If the devil cannot make you proud of your attainments in the flesh, he will make you proud that you are not proud of your attainments in the flesh. He can make you strut about your humility! Most of the problems with pride stem from false gauges that man has set up to measure maturity. Some equate being in demand with maturity. Other equate the possession of a certain gift or gifts of the Spirit with maturity. Still others assume that the more religious meetings we can attend, the more mature we are!

MATURITY IS THE SPIRIT OF JESUS REPRODUCED IN US MAKING US LIKE HIM. Try your maturity by that standard! He counted nothing he had too valuable to give up to become less than he was and give us heaven. He took upon himself the form of a servant and humbled himself and became obedient unto death . . . even the death of the cross. THAT IS MATURITY! Until we reach that state, we need not talk of maturity. There is none good!

Experience Versus Growth

Experience is meaningless, if it is not the *gateway* to *growth*. We have made grevious error to emphasize experience without growth. Likewise there can be no growth without proper bases. Often the bases of growth are not understood at all by the believer. He does not understand his position or his relationship with Christ. When the truth begins to dawn, he often will have a rather shocking experience. If experience is the end, it is certainly the "front end" of the adventure with Christ. When growth bases are recognized, growth patterns will develop.

Miles Stanford—in mentioning men God has used such as Tauler, Moody, Mueller, Trumbull, Hyde, Hopkins, and others— said, "The average for these was fifteen years after they entered their life work, before they began to know the Lord Jesus as their life, and ceased trying to work for Him and began allowing Him to be their all in all and do His work through them." He further says, "Certainly this is not to discount a Spirit-fostered experience, blessing, or even a crisis; but it is to be remembered that these simply contribute to the overall, and all-important process."

No experience or chain of experiences will do away with the need of growth in the Christian life. The world around us is evidence that in God's greatest works, He takes time and there are no shortcuts. Our physical growth is a clear illustration of how God works in our spiritual lives. Be patient with His processes.

Imbalance in Spiritual Things

It is painfully strange today that there are so many emphases, even with regard to the spiritual life, that many are left in confusion. During a recent tour of the space facilities in Florida, which took us into areas where few tourists were allowed to go, I was stricken with one word—BALANCE. Many companies work under one roof. The employees of these companies wear the insignias of the firm they represent. The final result of their work is a gigantic machine over thirty-five stories high with such amazing BALANCE that its behaviour can be predicted within a fraction of an inch, though it will travel multiplied thousands of miles.

Balance is the key! One worker may have one gift and another possesses quite a different gift. But they work together in respect of differing abilities. When the work is done, they look upon its wholeness, gratified to have been used in such a feat of efficiency. And when the gigantic machine roars into space, and every part

110

functions toward the success of the whole mission, all rejoice.

Revival has touched down in America! It has been no respector of age, class, culture, or denomination. It stands as a work of God through many kinds of people with many varied backgrounds and cultures, as well as religious traditions. Like the gigantic space machine, it bears the mark of much spiritual labor in prayer and intercession. It is not my revival, or yours, or theirs. It is HIS revival! Praise God that this is so!

Try to lean it in any direction or seek to exhibit the handiwork of one special group, and revival will abort before it goes into orbit. We stand in the same area of danger as Wales, when they capitulated to the devil in the midst of revival without knowing it. I quote from Jessie Penn-Lewis: "One of the most subtle things that the enemy ever did was when he turned the children of God in upon themselves to seek an inward experience of the baptism of the Holy Ghost, after the Welsh Revival. The advancing ranks of the Church were pressing on with a glorious shout of victory, when this subtle onslaught came from the enemy and checked it" (p. 38, *The Spiritual Warfare*).

It might be well to note that the disciples were first called. . . .
not Baptizers,
>not Charasmatics,
>>not Pentecostals,
not Deeper Life People,
>not Full Gospel Folks,
>>not even Children
>>of God
>not Glossalalists . . .

BUT CHRISTIANS! Their balance was such that they were not known for baptizing (though they did), or tongue-speaking (though they spoke in other languages), or for Pentecost (though that is where they surfaced with power), or anything else, but their undeniable likeness in character to Jesus Christ of Nazareth. WHEN YOU AND I WIN THE RIGHT BY CONDUCT AND CHARACTER TO WEAR THE NAME WE ALREADY CLAIM—CHRISTIAN—THERE WILL BE BALANCE! And

111

revival will move into nation-saving dimensions!

As long as the Spirit of God moves there will be menaces. The devil will see to that. But keep in mind that "If the Lord delight in us, then he will bring us into this land, and give it us; a land which floweth with milk and honey. Only rebel not ye against the Lord, neither fear ye the people of the land; FOR THEY ARE BREAD FOR US: their defence is departed from them, and the LORD IS WITH US: fear them not" (Num. 14:9). Every menace is a means of growth; every problem, a provision in embryo; every cloud, a challenge; and every high wall, an occasion to shout the victory!

13. The Law of Theodynamics

There are principles by which the spirit world operates just as there are principles by which the natural world operates. We call these "laws." A law is developed out of unvarying occurrences in any given area of truth.

The "law" of gravity, for instance, was advanced when a fellow got hit on the head by an apple falling from a tree. He asked himself why the apple had fallen downward and not upward. I don't know that he ever found out in terms that he could explain and I could understand, but he advanced a law which in effect stated that any given day, in any type of weather, under any given circumstances an apple which broke from its mooring in an apple tree would fall to the ground and not to the clouds.

One hundred apples could do the same under any circumstances. Unless some artificial force was exerted, they would fall to the ground or upon someone's head as the case might be. Thus, a law is born! The law existed long before it was stated. It was a help, however, to know that there was such a thing as gravity. Man could then put it to his use, rather than try to break it and find himself broken upon it.

I advance in this chapter a law which has been in force since the creation of the world and before! The knowledge of it will be of great benefit in *establishing* and *exerting* victory over the enemy. It will explain some mysteries as any law should do. It will open some areas of exciting study. Read this material deliberately and repeatedly, if necessary.

Definition of Terms

A law is an established principle, a reasonably anticipated procedure. A law is a rule of action or a uniform occurrence. What we are about to discuss is a law in proper context with these definitions.

"Theodynamics" is a word which is in nobody's dictionary and may never be—though perhaps it should be. My conviction is that when our civilization can stand nothing new, it is too old to exist. Therefore, I present to you a new word of my own coining—THEODYNAMICS. "Theos" in the Greek means "God." "Dunamis" in the Greek means "power." Thus we have the law of God-power. Thus the definition of the term is A PRINCIPLE GOVERNING EVIDENCES AND OCCURRENCES OF GOD'S POWER.

Detection of a Law

I didn't get hit on the head with an apple, but I did get a few bruises from the enemy and a few bruised feelings from my own powerless efforts. I began to put some facts together and found out something quite interesting. Listen to this line of thought: God is everywhere.

.God is God everywhere.

God is working as God everywhere.

The evidences of God's work are variable.

His power may be evident some places but not others.

I may back up and try to explain that one of the prior truths is not true. However, I cannot prove that they are not true. God is both omnipresent and omnipotent. He wants His will done everywhere. He has taught me to pray, "Thy Kingdom come, Thy will be done, on earth as it is in heaven." I believe that His power stands behind any prayer which He teaches me to pray.

My question is, "Why isn't His will being done everywhere." Further, why isn't it evident that his will is being done with the same degree of power everywhere? What is the variable or the reason for the variation in the evidences or demonstrations of His power? The answer lies in the negative forces at work in the world through the enemy, the devil.

The devil is not everywhere, but he knows about everywhere God is working. An intricate system of demons in places of responsibility is in touch with the whole scope of the work of God. Another vital question: Is the devil able in any given situation to oppose and overthrow a work of God or to stifle the display of His power? The answer is "NO!" But, we assert, the devil is able under some circumstances to smother a demonstration of God's power.

Right here we suspicion a principle. We discover that under one set of circumstances or after certain procedures spiritual victory is evident and God's power demonstrated. In the midst of other conditions, spiritual victory is always absent. Could it be that God has chosen to operate His spiritual laws of power according to certain divinely-chosen rules? I believe that the answer to this is "YES!" Let's state the law and discuss its facets.

Declaration of the Law

THE RELEASE AND EVIDENCE OF GOD'S POWER IS PROPORTIONATE TO THE SUCCESS OF THE PRAYERS OF THE RIGHTEOUS TO BIND THE RESISTANCE OF THE ENEMY AND CREATE CONDITIONS CONDUCIVE TO GOD'S WORKING. GOD CHOOSES TO LIMIT OR RELEASE HIS POWER IN A GIVEN AREA ACCORDING TO THE FREEDOM GRANTED BY THE PRAYERS OF HIS PEOPLE.

The law has many facets. It is a law which pertains to prayer as well as conduct. The dynamic of our praying and the deportment of our lives are factors which release the power of

114

God. There are many laws within this law, perticularly within the area of prayer. There is, for instance, the law of faith which says, "Whatsoever things ye desire when ye pray, BELIEVE that ye RECEIVE them and ye shall have them" (Mark 11:24).

It is a law which pertains to salvation. God is a God of salvation, and He is everywhere. People, however, are not being saved everywhere. Only when people pray and witness and individuals pray the prayer of faith are people saved. God's saving power is thrown into gear as the saints begin to pray in intercession.

It is a law which pertains to victory. God's victory is everywhere, because His power is everywhere. Not everyone, however, is living in victory. Only those who are receiving and believing in prayer have evidences of victory.

It is a law which pertains to power. God's power being everywhere, it is available. But as the sound waves filling the air can only be caught under certain conditions, so does His power become evident under certain conditions. "And when they prayed, the place was shaken" (Acts 4:31). Why was that particular place shaken? Because that is where they prayed!

Demonstrations of the Law

This law is demonstrated on virtually every page of the Bible. Signs of God's power were seemingly lost in the days of Noah, when man's rebellion was rampant. One man's faith, prayer, and conduct allowed God to move in a mighty demonstration of His power, as evidenced in the Flood. The devil's works were put down and judgment came.

God said many years later, "If my people, which are called by my name, shall humble themselves and pray and seek my face and turn from their wicked ways; then I will hear from heaven, and forgive their sins, and heal their land" (2 Chron. 7:14). God is saying that the spirit, prayers, diligence, and repentance of His people will cause Him to move upon the nation and redeem it!

Elijah had been ordered, "Go hide thyself!" This he did

115

without question. Again he was ordered, "Go shew thyself!" He obeyed again. As a result the people of the nation turned to God and shouted, "The Lord, He is God! The Lord, He is God!" God's power was released and a new day came for the nation. The Law of Theodynamics was demonstrated again.

You can study for yourself dozens of cases where this law is demonstrated. The devil's power is broken by prayer and the righteousness of God's people, and God's power is let loose!

Observe the early church and you see the law in effect. The phenomenon of Pentecost is a result of that Law in action. God did it out of His Sovereignty, but He still chose to use the factors He always used—the prayers of God's people and their condition of consecration. God will send His fire, but man must build the altars! And these altars must be built by divine dimensions and designations.

The Dynamics of the Law

It is the dynamic behind salvation as we have already stated. Salvation power is brought into being with the exercise of faith-praying. All of Satan's hindrances cannot keep God from getting through when the sinner prays.

It is the dynamic behind the fulness of the Spirit. Jesus promised this fulness when certain qualifications were met. When we thirst, come, drink, and believe—God responds with the overflow from the outflow. RIVERS OF LIVING WATERS WOULD FLOW FROM WITHIN BECAUSE OF THE SUPPLY OF THE HOLY SPIRIT! Obey the Law of Theodynamics. God in any given time or place, under any circumstances, will release from within you the same rivers of living waters.

This law is the dynamic behind revival. We have heard God's revival promise in 2 Chronicles 7:14. That is a timeless promise. Let's restate the law with reference to revival in our day: THE RELEASE AND EVIDENCE OF GOD'S POWER IS PROPORTIONATE TO THE SUCCESS OF THE PRAYERS OF THE RIGHTEOUS TO BIND THE RESISTANCE OF THE

ENEMY, AND CREATE CONDITIONS CONDUCIVE TO GOD'S WORKING.

WHEN WE GET ON PRAYING GROUND BY HUMBLING OURSELVES,

THEN PRAY THE PRAYER OF FAITH,

SEEKING GOD'S FACE,

REPENTING OF OUR SINS AND TURNING FROM THEM,

THEN . . . THE LAW GOES INTO EFFECT AND REVIVAL COMES!

That law tells us that we can bind something on earth and it will be bound in heaven (Matt. 18:18). Earth's prayers have heavenly effect! It does matter that you and I pray! It matters greatly how we live and what we say! It is of universal and eternal significance that God has chosen to operate with His glorious power within the framework of our praying and living.

GOD, RELEASE US TO RELEASE YOU!

14. The Power of the Spoken Word

Our victory over the devil in the final analysis will be a matter of tapping the power of God available to His people. That power is all around us. We live in a power-filled universe. We are told that there is enough power latent in a cubic foot of air to blow the largest city off the face of the earth. There is enough power in one atom to begin a chain reaction that would wrap the world in a blanket of fire. God has charged the world with power. That power was to be used for man's blessings and God's glory. That power was set in motion by words. That power can be controlled by words.

A World Made with Words

"Through faith, we understand that the worlds were framed by the WORD OF GOD . . . so that things which are seen are not

117

made of things which do appear" (Heb. 11:3). The creative process of God, whatever the detail, was brought about by HIS SPOKEN WORD. He said it and it was so. He spoke it and it stood steadfast. Listen to the record:

"And God *said,* Let there be light: and there was light" (Gen. 1:3).

"And God *said,* Let there be a firmament" (Gen. 1:6).

"And God *said,* Let the waters under the heaven be gathered unto one place, and let the dry land appear; and it was so" (Gen. 1:9).

"And God *said,* Let the earth bring forth grass, the herb yielding seed, and the fruit tree yielding fruit after his kind, whose seed is in itself, upon the earth; and it was so" (Gen. 1:11).

"And God *said,* Let there be lights in the firmament of the heaven to divide the day from the night; and let them be for signs, and for seasons, and for days, and years" (Gen. 1:14).

"And God *said,* Let the waters bring forth abundantly the moving creature that hath life, and fowl that may fly above the earth in open firmament of heaven" (Gen. 1:20).

"And God *said,* Let the earth bring forth the living creature after his kind, cattle, and creeping thing, and beast of the earth after his kind; and it was so" (Gen. 1:24).

"And God *said,* Let us make man in our own image, after our likeness; and let him have dominion over the fish of the sea, and over the fowl of the air, and over all the earth, and over every creeping thing that creepeth upon the earth" (Gen. 1:26).

God spoke, and there was creation. What He said became reality. All that we see about us in the created world was made by a word from God. The creation is His spoken word materialized.

A World Controlled by Words

God not only made a world with words, but He made a world which could be controlled and influenced by words. He made man so that he could speak words and gave him dominion over everything that He had made. That dominion covered all the created world. Man reigned in that world under the authority of God. As God spoke and man obeyed, man spoke and the world obeyed. It was a world of word-power. What man heard God say, he repeated and the world responded. We do not know how he tended the garden, but we can be sure that it did not involve the back-breaking, frustrating work that a twentieth century gardener faces. I have a conviction that it was a garden that responded to the words of the gardener. He spoke and there was beauty, just as his Creator had done. He was endowed with Godlike capacities.

The World Fell Because of a Word

Along came the devil. He introduced the first doubt and presented the first lie. But the world did not fall, until man chose to believe the devil. Man and woman spoke a word, which was not in agreement with their Creator. They sinned in the act of independence, and they fell. The earth fell with them. Dominion was lost to man. When man forfeited his dominion, the devil cashed in on it. Man had believed in the word of the devil and confessed it in action. The result was chaos and confusion. The first Adam had failed!

The Word Became Flesh

"In the beginning was the Word, and the Word was with God, and the Word was God." A word is thought crystallized. Jesus is all that God ever thought in human form. The word give definition to the thought. Jesus is God's thought defined. He was the Creative Agency in the universe. "All things were made by him; and without him was not made anything that was made" (John 1:3).

"And the Word was made flesh, and dwelt among us, and we beheld his glory, (the glory as of the only begotten of the Father,) full of grace and truth" (John 1:14).

We see in Jesus Christ the power of the spoken word personified. We begin to see through the ministry of Jesus the awesome power of the spoken word.

119

To the winds and waves He said, "Peace be still!"

To the demons in the man in the synagogue He said, "Hush and leave."

To the fever He gave vocal rebuke, and it obeyed.

To the fig tree He gave a curse and it died, drying up from the roots.

To the nobleman He said, "Go thy way, thy son is alive."

To the cripple, He said, "Take up thy bed and walk."

To the leper He said, "Be thou clean."

He cast out demons with a word and healed the people with a word.

The power that the Father had in creation, He had given the Son. He could speak something into reality with a word.

The centurion in Mathew 8:8 discovered the great mystery which many have never found when he said, "Lord, I am not worthy that you should come under my roof: BUT SPEAK THE WORD ONLY AND MY SERVANT SHALL BE HEALED." And it was so!

Having What You Say

One day Jesus and his disciples were walking along and He came to a fig tree with leaves. Upon finding no figs on the tree, He simply said, "No man eat fruit of thee hereafter for ever" (Mark 11:14). I wonder what the disciples thought when they heard their Master talking to a tree. The next morning when they passed by it, the tree was dead, having dried up from the roots. Peter said, "Master, the fig tree which you cursed is withered away."

Now, have you ever asked yourself just why Jesus would do such a thing? It was certainly not that He was vindictive. What did He have against fig trees? And why did He speak to the tree? First, we see divine displeasure with fruitlessness. Then we see the sheer power of a word spoken in faith. The life in the tree responded to the words of Jesus and could not live before those words. He would use this illustration to teach His disciples a great—unforgettable lesson.

He said in response to Peter's reminder, "Have faith in God" (Mark 11:22). (Literally, "Have the God kind of faith.") Then He said, "For verily I say unto you, that whosoever shall SAY to this MOUNTAIN, Be thou removed, and be cast into the sea; and shall not doubt in his heart, but shall believe that those things which he saith shall come to pass; HE SHALL HAVE WHATSOEVER HE SAITH" (Mark 11:23). He was literally saying, "YOU WILL HAVE WHAT YOU SAY!" What a glorious and frightening declaration.

Jesus said much the same thing in Luke 17:6, "If ye had faith as a grain of mustard seed, ye might say unto this sycamine tree, Be thou plucked up by the roots, and be thou planted in the sea; and it should obey you."

He said in Matthew 17:20, when the disciples questioned as to why they could not cast out the demon in the lad, "Because of your unbelief; for verily I say unto you, If ye have faith as a grain of mustard seed, ye shall say to this mountain, Remove hence to yonder place; and it shall remove; and nothing shall be impossible to you."

A Faith That Talks to Mountains and Trees

Jesus had talked to a tree. The tree responded to His word by dying. He had cursed it with a word. There was power in His spoken word. He then suggested that if they spoke to a mountain, telling it to be removed and cast into the sea, if they believed without doubting, they would have what they said.

Now, I have purposely looked in the yellow pages of the phone directory and never found a company that existed for the purpose of moving mountains. I can't think of anything more difficult than to move a mountain. A mountain is a symbol of power in the Bible. Yet by the word of faith any mountain can be removed or any tree plucked up by the roots. Jesus does not expect us to stop at considering mountains and trees, but powers of the devil and obstacles to Christian progress. If He can move mountains, He can move problems and illnesses, worries, and heartaches.

121

If this faith can converse with mountains and trees, it can certainly converse with Satan and his demons. As our spoken words line up with the written Word of God, there is power.

By Words We Are Justified or Condemned

Jesus affirms that, "Every idle word that men shall speak, they shall give account thereof in the day of judgment. For by thy words thou shalt be justified, and by thy words thou shalt be condemned" (Matt. 12:36-37). Why is there such value in words? Words give life or death, blessing or cursing. No wonder that the wise man said, "A wholesome tongue is a tree of life" (Prov. 15:4). He further said, "Thou art snared with the words of thy mouth, thou art taken with the words of thy mouth" (Prov. 6:2). He gives the promise, "A man's belly shall be satisfied with the fruit of his mouth; and with the increase of his lips shall he be filled" (Prov. 18:20).

We are saved by confession. "But what saith it? The word is nigh thee, even in thy mouth, and in thy heart; that is, the word of faith, which we preach. That if thou shalt confess with thy mouth the Lord Jesus, and believe in thine heart that God hath raised Him from the dead, THOU SHALT BE SAVED" (Rom. 10:8-9).

By Words We Are Blessing or Cursing

The tongue is an explosive tool. It sets on fire the circle of nature. It is equivalent in the unseen world to a chain reaction from an atomic explosion in the physical world. If we could understand that statement, what an effect it would have on our use of the tongue. James further says of the tongue, "Therewith bless we God, even the Father; and therewith curse we men, which are made after the similitude of God. Out of the same mouth cometh forth *blessing* and *cursing*." Our words are either used of the devil to curse or by the Lord to bless. Men giving a bad confession place curses on themselves and those around them. Folks who are making positive confessions, that is in line with God's Word, bless men and God by their words.

We Are Ever Confessing

We never rise above our confession. We are what we confess. If we confess illness, we are ill. If we confess fatigue, we are tired. If we confess fear, we are fearful. If we confess doubt, we are filled with unbelief. If we confess strength, we are strong. If we confess certainty, we are filled with belief. If we confess health, we are well. Jesus said, "You will have what you say" (Mark 11:23). The word for "confess" is an interesting word. It is a combination of two words, one meaning "the same" and the other meaning "to say." Literally it means "to say the same." More literally, it means sameness with Jesus, because He is the Word, LOGOS. To confess, then, means to say the same with Jesus.

What Happens When We Make a Good Confession?

Jesus says, "Whosoever therefore shall confess me before men, him will I also confess before my Father which is in heaven. But whosoever shall deny me before men, him will I also deny before my Father which is in heaven" (Matt. 10:32-33). Jesus is the High Priest of our profession (confession). When we make a good confession that is one which agrees with the Word of God, Jesus takes that confession before the Father and presents it to Him. The Father then releases the powers of heaven to make that confession a reality. Jesus is our advocate with the Father, presenting our confession to the Father for certification. He can only present what we give Him to present. "Seeing then that we have a great High Priest, that is passed into the heavens, Jesus the Son of God *let us hold fast our profession* [confession]" (Heb. 4:14).

When we confess Jesus in the midst of a situation, He confesses us and the Father validates all we confessed. If we give no positive confession, our High Priest has nothing to say.

What Happens When We Make a Bad Confession?

Satan's word is as false as God's Word is true. When we agree with Satan's word, that is a bad confession. When we agree with the circumstances and do not see through eyes of faith, we make a confession that Satan can use. We may murmur and complain, ridicule or criticize. When we do the devil picks up on it immediately and appears before the throne to accuse us to God and God to us. Our High Priest, Jesus, has nothing to say. We have given Him nothing to take to the Father. The devil flings our bad confession in the face of the Father and then activates his demons to make real what we said! The devil is given authority before God by our bad confessions.

An Example of Good Confession

When the angel spoke to Mary, he told her a story that was beyond her ability to understand. But faith treads in areas where understanding never walks. She responded by saying, "Be it unto me according to thy word" (Luke 1:38). In that word of faith she loosed the blessings of heaven. The highest degree that can be was conferred upon her. "Blessed is she that believed; FOR THERE SHALL BE A PERFORMANCE OF THOSE THINGS WHICH WERE TOLD HER FROM THE LORD" (Luke 1:45). Mary made a good confession, and it was validated before the court of heaven and realized in the earth.

What Are You Confessing Now?

We have what we confess. We are what we confess. The world has heard our confessions of failure and weakness. Let it hear, now, the confession of faith in Jesus, our victory and Victor. Let us confess our strength in Him, and He, our High Priest, will make it real before the court of heaven.

Confess right now . . . Christ now lives in me. He is strong. I belong no longer in the ranks of failure. I can do all things through Christ, which strengtheneth me. He is my life. He gives me His ability. I have been delivered from the powers of darkness and have been translated into His Kingdom where He is Lord! He is at this moment at work in me willing and working His good pleasure. He is now meeting every need that is mine according to His riches in glory. I am filled with the Living Word and believing according to the written Word that He is now giving me the victory. How we need to build testimonies on the Word and rehearse them before the world, before the Lord, and before the devil.

Every one of us should have one Bible marked so that every promise is personalized. Take a few of the precious promises and put your name wherever there is an opportunity. For instance, Let *Jim's* character or moral disposition be free from the love of money, including greed, avarice, lust, and craving for earthy possessions . . . and be satisfied with his present circumstances and with what he has. For he himself [God] hath said, " 'I WILL NOT LEAVE *JIM* WITHOUT SUPPORT. I WILL NOT, I WILL NOT, I WILL NOT IN ANY DEGREE LEAVE JIM HELPLESS, NOR FORSAKE *JIM,* NOR LET HIM DOWN, NOR RELAX MY HOLD ON HIM, ASSUREDLY NOT! SO I TAKE COMFORT AND AM ENCOURAGED, AND CONFIDENT AND BOLDLY SAY, THE LORD IS MY HELPER, I WILL NOT BE SEIZED WITH ALARM . . . I WILL NOT FEAR OR DREAD OR BE TERRIFIED. WHAT CAN MAN DO TO ME?" (Heb. 13:5-6, Amplified Version).

The power of the spoken word is an indispensable tool in our victory over the devil. When we confess in accord with the Word of God, the devil must retreat. All of Heaven's power is then released to do God's bidding in our lives.

A Good Confession

HE dwells in me,
HE dwells in me,
The Mighty One now dwells in me,
He makes Himself a reality
This Mighty One who lives in me.
HE dwells in me,
HE dwells in me,
The Risen One now dwells in me,
His resurrection power gives me

This Risen One has set me free.
    HE reigns in me,
    HE reigns in me,
The Coming One now reigns in me,
The Lord of Life HE is to me,
This Coming One will come for me.

15. What Is That in Thine Hand?

We now come to the last chapter of this volume and the most important. It poses a question, the answer to which will decide for you the issue of victory.

I want you to relive with me an exciting drama in the life of Moses—the pivotal hour of his life. You know the story of Moses. He was born in a day when Hebrew boy babies were not welcome in the kingdom of Egypt. He was born under a sentence of death. His innovating mother hid him in a waterproof basket among the flags in the river.

To this river, the daughter of Pharaoh came to wash herself. She saw the basket and sent her maid to fetch it. When she opened the basket, she saw the baby and loved him. The sister of the baby had been watching the basket and came to ask if she could not go and find a nurse for the child. She then went for the baby's very own mother who raised him, being paid wages from Egypt's treasury for the job. Pharaoh's daughter called him Moses, because he was taken from the water.

Thus, the providence of God would have it that the deliverer of God's children grew up right under the devil's nose, his fare paid for from the devil's treasury. He grew up in palace surroundings, palace finery, and palace culture. He possessed palace persuasion and received the finest education money could buy. When he was grown, he looked upon the burdens of his people. He saw an Egyptian mistreating one of his brethren, whereupon he slew the Egyptian and hid him in the sand.

Failure in the Flesh

Alas, the winds of God always blow to soon expose the works of the flesh. For the next day Moses saw two of his brethren striving and offered his help. His help was rejected and he was informed that they knew the mystery of the missing Egyptian. Frightened, Moses immediately fled from the face of Pharaoh and dwelt in the land of Midian. Stephen in his historic discourse in Acts 7, gives us more detail on the life of Moses. He spent forty years on the backside of the wilderness, a highly educated man, herding sheep! He had failed!

Now, there was every reason to believe that Moses had all the qualifications for success. He certainly was not short on desire and enthusiasm. He could have surely been voted "most likely to succeed" in his class. But he failed. And the flesh will always fail. So we follow him to the wilderness with degrees from Egypt's finest universities and connections the noblest would covet.

There in the wilderness, he begins work on another degree. It takes some folks longer than others to get this one. It took Moses forty years. I call it the "B.N." Degree—the "Be Nothing" Degree. He already had his "B.S." Degree—his "Be Something" Degree. How often God has to expose us to the humblest of surroundings before we will learn to be nothing so that He might be everything.

Second Call to Victory

When this "Be Nothing" Degree was fully earned and conferred, God was ready to call Moses for the task at which he had failed before. God designed a burning bush and sent his angel issuing Moses a clarified call. I feel certain that as God explained His call to Moses and presented His promises for success, Moses was going back in his mind to forty years ago. Then, there was no reason why he should fail. Did he not have all the furnishings for success? Did he not have palace education, palace culture, and palace persuasion?

127

Now, there was no reason why he should succeed. His degrees had yellowed with age and turned up at the edges. His expensive suits had long since tattered and were thrown away. His oratory and persuasion had lost the polish. And yet God issued to him the second call.

When God was through with his presentation, Moses answered with a most valid excuse. "But, behold, they will not believe me nor hearken unto my voice; for they will say, The Lord hath not appeared unto thee" (Ex. 4:1). This is a consideration that every child of God should have. We should be careful lest there not be about our lives those necessary credentials that prove that we have been with God. God had presented His call, and now Moses presents his excuse.

A Vital Visual Aid

Then a most unusual drama folows. I have read it for years without ever seeing the significance of it, but I have recently found that tucked just beneath the surface of this narative is a principle that is priceless in the life of victory.

God asks a strange question, "What is that in thine hand?" (Ex. 4:2). The simple answer was, "A rod." God's quick request came back, "Cast it on the ground." Now I believe that surely at least in the mind of Moses there was a conversation with the Lord. "But Lord, this is a fine tool and it has been nothing to me but advantageous. I don't see the value of throwing it down." "Moses I didn't ask you to see anything, I asked you to throw it down."

"But Lord, it has guided me over uneven paths and protected the flocks from wild animals. In fact it has become a real companion to me, sort of a security image." "Throw it down, Moses."

Reluctantly he threw it down, and it immediately became a writhing, hissing serpent right before his eyes. The Scripture simply says, "And Moses fled from before it" (Ex. 4:3). The fact was he took off in a dash! By the time God spoke again, he was surely a hundred yards away.

The Lord then said, "Moses, come back and pick it up—by

the tail." Now throwing down a dead rod was one thing. Picking up a live snake was quite another! I think he might even have asked God to repeat that command. He heard it right the first time! I think he must have slowly sauntered back to the original scene with hands in pockets hoping against hope that the reptile would be gone by the time he got there. But it was still there in living color! "Lord, that is a snake." "Pick it up, Moses, by the tail." Now everyone knows if you are going to pick up a snake and hold it, you want to hold it by the business end. Holding the snake by the tail leaves the dangerous end unattended. But God is saying, "Obey me and take the lesser end. I will take care of the rest."

More reluctantly than he dropped it, he picked it up. The serpent became a rod again in his hand; "That they may believe that the Lord God of their fathers, the God of Abraham, the God of Isaac, and the God of Jacob, hath appeared unto thee." End of narrative. Beginning of mystery. Why did he do it? What did it all mean? These and other questions will be answered as we proceed. Let us go on!

God Starts with Where We Are

God wants your attention right where you are. You would desire to get to another point of life. It will always be like this, until you are divinely cornered. God begins with the *here* and *now!* WHAT *IS* THAT IN THINE HAND? It isn't a matter of what is going to be or what has been—WHAT *IS?* He starts with what you have. It may be a simple rod, but it is a place to start. You would wait until you possess something more, but He starts with what you now hold in your hand. That is where He will start with you.

God Wants Us to Put It Down

There is about anything which we have not put down before the Lord the nature of the serpent present. The old uncrucified self-life is there coiled like a poisonous snake ready to inject the deadly poison. We can recount many a person like Moses who possessed singular abilities, but never threw them down before the Lord. Many of them have joined the wreckage along the way. What is that in your hand? Throw it down! If it is worth having God will give it back to us cleansed. If He does not give it back, it will be because He has something better.

Do you hesitate to throw it down? Is there good reason? Do you suspicion that you love that which you hold in your hand more than you love Him? You don't really have it anyway, until you have it in Him. It will not advantage you or Him until it is His. As long as you have it, there will be no more power exercised through it than you have. That rod in the hand of Moses could do no more work than Moses could; it had no more power than Moses had; it could accomplish no more than Moses could accomplish.

As Moses put it before the Lord, its true nature came out. There is a snake in everything that we have not thrown down before the Lord. It does not come out until God has a chance to deal with it.

That They May Believe

"Now, Moses pick it up by the tail." "Lord, do you realize that this is a snake?" "Yes, Moses, I said pick it up—by the tail." "I sure hope you know what you are doing, Lord!" Moses picked up the snake and lo and behold it became a rod again in his hand. "THAT THEY MAY BELIEVE . . . THAT GOD HAS APPEARED UNTO YOU" (Ex. 4:5). "But what will make them feel like believing?" Moses must feel like asking. We shall see. The first visual lesson is finished, and Moses holds the rod in his hand.

What Is the Rod?

This rod is destined to become the most famous rod in history. What does it symbolize? It is obvious that it symbolizes the life that is Spirit-anointed. It depicts the authority that God commits to human hands. Here is one of the clearest Old Testament pictures of the experience of Spirit-fulness. God's promise follows,

"And thou shalt take this rod in thine hand, wherewith thou shalt do *signs*" (Ex. 4:17).

This is now the rod of yieldedness, the rod of abandonment, THE ROD OF GOD. Until now it was just a rod in the hand of a man. It could do no more than a man could do. It had no more power than the man who held it. It reflected more his weakness than strength. It had not been used to accomplish one miracle until now. BUT NOW IT IS THE ROD OF GOD! (Ex. 4:20). This rod would become a symbol of Heaven's awesome power, of God's might.

Moses now held in his hand the symbol of divine authority . . . God's authority over him and his authority under God.

It will do you good to note that in a matter of days Moses and his brother, Aaron, discredited the whole theological system of Egypt. They could have advanced arguments, held study courses, and talked themselves blue-faced for a hundred years and have failed to budge the stern system of gods and goddesses. But with the anointing of God upon them, their rods, they turned the trick in a matter of a few short weeks. Moses stretched that rod out again and again, and God's judgment came like a mighty wave across the land. Finally Pharaoh seemed beaten and capitulated. The Israelites began their trek to freedom.

Authority That Will Liberate from Bondage

Soon, Israel reaches to the Red Sea, a real obstacle. Pharaoh and his army are coming up from behind. The people begin to murmur. Moses stands up and declares, "Fear ye not, stand still, and see the salvation of the Lord, which he shall show you today." Then Moses goes to prayer, but God stops him short. "Wherefore criest thou unto me. Speak unto the children of Israel, that they may go forward: BUT LIFT THOU UP THY ROD!" (Ex. 14:15-16). Moses was about to ask God to do something. God said, in effect, "Moses, do it yourself." He would now try the authority that was his. What did that rod mean? Moses was not his own. That group of griping people were not his, nor Pharaoh and his army. It simply was not his problem, but God's! Praise the Lord!

Moses asserted his authority, lifting up the rod. The sea divided, and the children of Israel went across on dry ground. They moved out of bondage. When the Spirit takes over, He will move you out of bondage.

Authority That Will Supply Needs

The next crisis was a water shortage. They simply ran out. How soon do people forget the prior provisions of God! They began to murmur. "Wherefore is this that thou hast brought us up out of Egypt, to kill us and our children and our cattle with thirst." So intense were they in their anger that Moses despaired for his very life. "Lord, what shall I do unto this people? They be almost ready to stone me." (Most every pastor at one time or another have been in a position to sympathize with Moses!)

God's answer came in a command to take some elders and go to the rock Horeb and smite it with THE ROD. Moses had fresh memories of smiting things with that rod with resulting bruises. Have we not all known the experience of beating on things with the rods of fleshly strength to find it frustratingly painful? But remember this is now the ROD OF GOD. It can hit as hard as God can hit. It has the potential of its proper Owner! When God hits a thing, something has to give! The rock is smitten and a river of life-giving water flows out to meet the needs of the people and to spare. Those who act under Spirit-authority will find all their needs supplied!

Authority That Will Defeat Our Enemy

Then came the enemy! Amalek stood in the middle of their path in Exodus 17:8 and said, "You have gone far enough!" Moses doesn't even stutter. He orders Joshua to the valley to prepare for battle, and he proposes to stand on the hill with THE ROD OF GOD IN MINE HAND (Ex. 17:9). He is catching on at long last. He is beginning to understand walking in the Spirit. He is beginning to discover the adventure of spiritual authority. There can be no more power in the valley of service and warfare than there is exerted in the prayer closet or on the hill. As long as Moses declares authority, Joshua prevails and Amalek retreats. But when his hands were heavy and the rod was lowered, Amalek prevailed and Joshua retreated.

Here is a simple formula. Walk in the Spirit and you will not fulfill the lusts of the flesh (Gal. 5:16). Live in your authority, continue in the Spirit's filling, and your enemy must retreat. Let down for a moment and the tide of battle turns. At last Aaron and Hur come to the rescue. And how often we thus need each other. They took a stone and put it under Moses and held his hands steady, until the going down of the sun. AND THE VICTORY WAS WON. The Spirit-controlled life will defeat the enemy!

What Is That in Your Hand?

What are you holding? An image of yourself? A promising career? A successful ministry? A family? A degree? Put it down before the Lord!

Would you walk in the authority of another world? Then, walk in the Spirit's power. It would be better to lose all and gain His power than to have all and be powerless. We will never possess the power of God except by the lesser end. It is God's power, and we hold it lightly. It will never be ours, but as it is His and ours in His will. It could be withdrawn without a moment's notice. It is tragic to have to remind you that this mighty power later was the occasion for a shortened life when Moses resorted to a selfish tantrum and misused the rod. It cost him the promised land and many years of fruitful life.

Would you not, before you lay this volume aside, put down all that you have before the Lord. That's right, everything! Put down your business, your ministry, your plans, your abilities, your family, your usefulness, your schedule, your esteem in the community, your plan to make a million. Put it all down. Dare to stand before Him stripped of all that was yours in order to be endued with all that is His!

The result will be that you will have a life before which seas open, rocks split, and enemies retreat. You will have the power of God upon your life. YOU WILL HAVE VICTORY OVER THE DEVIL.

> Our Lord has Satan conquered,
>> His stronghold entered in,
> And broken his dominion,
>> Thank God, we're free from sin!
> The long, long night is ended,
>> And freedom's morn is here,
> We sing our songs of triumph,
>> Our hearts are free from fear.
>> *HALLELUJAH!*